"In this compelling collection, Jana Harris, poet and longtime research-
er of the pioneer era, imagines and animates the voices of 19th-century
women as they adapt to the frontiers of marriage and the American West.
While Harris's vivid language and imagery offer more than enough plea-
sures to delight and sustain the reader, it is her remarkably intuitive grasp
of individual lives (inner and outer) that makes this book an exceptional,
complex realization of time, place and experience. It might be said Harris
has written a novel in poems—a novel one can't put down."
—Ann McCutchan, author of *River Music: An Atchafalaya Story* and
Circular Breathing: Meditations from a Musical Life

"Harris is the bard of pioneer women's voices in the Northwest and
now...it is clear that she is speaking for a vast American experience in
the nineteenth century, one that resonates to this very day.... 'Who can
account,' she writes in her rendering of the voice of Lucy Stevens from
Oregon, 1875, 'for what catches in memory's cogs?' It is the American
experience that has caught in Harris' cogs and here she gives it back to us
in all its glory."—Janet Sternburg, author of, *Phantom Limb*; *White Mat-
ter: A Memoir of Family and Medicine*; *The Writer on Her Work*

"In poems at once accessible and deep, Jana Harris brings to vibrant life
the women who pioneered the Pacific Northwest. While they faced an
array of common struggles, in Harris's wise telling they emerge nonethe-
less as unforgettable individuals."—Suzanne Lebsock, author of
A Murder in Virginia: Southern Justice on Trial

"*You Haven't Asked About My Wedding or What I Wore* is both a wrenching
history lesson and a lyrical celebration of courage. Jana Harris writes with
complexity and passion about the difficult lives of nineteenth century
girls and women living in the west or heading there. Quebecois nuns,
Black slaves, Native Americans, Euro-Americans—all these women trav-
el from their homes in search of better lives. The narrative poems, based
on assiduous research about real women, dramatize hope, struggle, infant
mortality, illness, early marriage and, occasionally, satisfaction. Other
poems feature lists of survival tools or the small comforts that make life
bearable on the frontier. The women's fortitude and resilience are beau-
tifully summed up by Elizabeth Gay, 'I sang or hummed/nobody died as
long as there was music.'—Valerie Miner, author of *Traveling with Spirits*

"Jana Harris is an absolute original. Nobody has her clarity, her liveliness and oh that unmistakable voice! [This book] is a marvel of storytelling and a totally unique way of breathing life into stuffy archives, making women's lives hum, with its acute sense of place and language. It's a thrilling, daring work."—Louise Bernikow, author of *Among Women* and *Dreaming in Libro: How a Good Dog Tamed a Bad Woman*

"Harris resurrects a host of women (and men) from the distant past (the century before last) and lets them have their say, this time about the lost customs of courtship and marriage. Their voices, each distinct but part of a mesmerizing whole, bring an entire bygone world to life. Harris does this with seeming effortlessness. Finely detailed, thoroughly engaging, and unexpectedly moving (goose bumps and tears not uncommon), these poems are a singular achievement."—David Trinidad, author of *Dear Prudence: New and Selected Poems* and *Peyton Place: A Haiku Soap Opera*

"Diligently researched from lists, diaries, letters, hymns, recipes and other authentic archival sources, [Harris's] poems expose stark realities epitomized by this dialog between Sarah Jane Sturgess, 13-year old land claim bride and her prospective husband, William Reese Anderson:
> It's best, he says, to name children
> after generals to give them courage. What
> about the girls? I say."
—Joan Maiers author of *Tcha Teemanwi*

You Haven't Asked About
My Wedding or What I Wore

You Haven't Asked About My Wedding or What I Wore

*Poems of Courtship
on the North American Frontier*

by Jana Harris

University of Alaska Press
Fairbanks

SNOWY OWL BOOKS
an imprint of the University of Alaska Press
P.O. Box 756240
Fairbanks, AK 99775-6240

Library of Congress Cataloging-in-Publication Data

You haven't asked me about my wedding or what I wore : poems of courtship & mar-
riage on the American frontier / by Jana Harris.
    pages cm
  Includes bibliographical references.
  ISBN 978-1-60223-235-8 (pbk. : alk. paper) — ISBN 978-1-60223-236-5 (ebook)
  1. Marriage—Poetry. 2. Courtship—Poetry. 3. Frontier and pioneer life—West
(U.S.)—Poetry. 4. Frontier and pioneer life—Canada, Western—Poetry. 5. Ameri-
can poetry—Women authors—19th century. 6. Poetry, American—19th century.
7. Women pioneers—Biography. I. Harris, Jana, 1947– editor of compilation.
II. Title: Poems of courtship & marriage on the American frontier.
  PS595.M3Y68 2014
  811.008'03543—dc23
                    2013049756

Cover design by Tina Kachele
Cover photo: John Cogswell and Mary Frances (Mamie) Gay on their wedding day,
October 28, 1852. Lane County [Oregon] Historical Museum.

This publication was printed on acid-free paper that meets the minimum require-
ments for ANSI / NISO Z39.48–1992 (R2002) (Permanence of Paper for Printed
Library Materials).

Printed in the United States

In memory of my beloved editors: Raymond J. Smith (1930-2008) and Harry J. Smith (1936-2012), cornerstones of the American small press movement of the later twentieth century, without which these pages would never have been written.

Contents

Illustrations

Foreword

During my more than thirty years of reading reminiscences, diaries, and letters of forgotten North American pioneer women, one shining narrative continues to leap out at me: Amid these ladies' hard lives, their most sterling memories were often either their courtship and wedding or the courtship and wedding of a family member. It was a given that a nineteenth-century bride-to-be's marriage ceremony was the focal point of her life, that she was the center of attention without having to commit the unladylike transgression of putting herself forward. Ironically this young woman, who most likely hauled water in a wooden bucket from creek to house and then wore her knees raw scrubbing splintery floors (if indeed she was lucky enough to live in a home that had a floor) dreamed of a wedding shaped by nothing American but by the British queen Victoria's marriage in 1840 to her cousin, Albert.

Victoria's white church wedding—publicized for years afterward—infected the minds of young women everywhere. According to nineteenth-century women's magazines, Victoria's hair was ringed with garlands of orange blossoms, setting a trend that other brides follow to this day. Until 1840 most American women married at home, but suddenly church weddings became more popular. *Women's Indispensable Assistant, Harper's Weekly,* and *Godey's Lady's Book,* a monthly magazine, touted nuptial accoutrements. Victoria raised five daughters, and with the marriage of each princess, attention by the press to wedding accoutrements was refreshed. Myrtle flowers, the botanical symbol of Aphrodite, became a wedding staple. Victoria and Albert were contemporaries and enormous fans of Felix Mendelssohn. The wedding of the Princess Royal in 1858 was possibly the first time that Mendelssohn's "Wedding March"—written for Shakespeare's *Midsummer Night's Dream*—was played at a nuptial rite, the beginning of a long tradition. To the end of the 1800s and beyond, American brides followed the nuptial fashions of British royalty.

As she looked out the doorless entry of her parents' lean-to, a North American frontier girl had such dreams in front of her. Who she married framed the whole rest of her life. Indeed, a nineteenth-century bride-to-be referred to getting married as "trying her fortune." She wore her best dress if she had one, if not she borrowed. Until the late 1800s, it was probably not white, though after the Civil War, she might have worn a white headpiece or a tiara with a white veil and carried flowers from her mother's garden. If it was winter, then cloth blooms made by the local milliner sufficed.

If, indeed, her dress was white, she might later dye it a darker hue so that she could wear it again, or she might save the wealth of fabric to cut into diapers and bibs for her firstborn. If life took a heartbreaking turn, the material could be used to line her infant's coffin.

If she wasn't married at home—usually too small a dwelling to host a wedding during inclement weather—then she probably wed in a community structure that served as church, school, and meeting hall. Her marriage would be officiated by the visiting preacher who passed through a few times a month, and her rites often combined into the scheduled church service.

For most of the nineteenth century, the only wedding music, other than Mendelssohn, was traditional hymns of comfort, faith, and fidelity sung by the congregation, often without organ accompaniment. Then, just before the dawn of a new century, the comic opera *Robin Hood* debuted in Chicago and featured the song "Oh Promise Me." The lyrics struck a chord in the public consciousness and were immediately incorporated into nuptial rites, both religious and nonreligious. The song remains a wedding staple to this day.

As I studied interviews of nineteenth-century frontier women conducted during the 1920s and '30s, I noted that courtship and marriage was often the lens through which the subject reported her life—though this was not always the framework the interviewer had in mind. I began to imagine the voices of these women as they looked back on the day they tried their fortune, sometimes with a man they hardly knew.

Queen Victoria marries Prince Albert of Saxe-Coburg and Gotha, 1840. Queen Victoria and Prince Albert mark the anniversary of their February 10, 1840, wedding with this re-creation of the day on May 11, 1854.

The Gift of a Found Half Moon

Mary Hallen, Western Ontario, Canada, 1850

She was our cousin, he our neighbor;
we wanted to give them something.
Eleanora said I could take a swatch of her
corn-colored hair for making macramé.
But we'd no way to frame it. We'd no money
so silver napkin ring, crystal pitcher,
a tablecloth out of the question.
Some embroidery perhaps, but we'd only
white cotton thread and precious little of it.
Eleanora, good with likenesses, but
we'd no paper (even if we had pen
and ink) or canvas, and the only color
we might use as paint, gentian violet
for marking sheep. We had smooth stones used
as bed warmers—they'd saved what's left
of Papa's ears, blackened by frostbite, peeling
like Mandarin rind. Our stones
somehow too precious to give up.

                    Eleanora
found it—a white half-moon growing on
a weeping hemlock trunk. Brought it home and
with hardwood sticks scratched upon its canvas.
Later when dried, Oh, the likenesses of us
standing in our yard: our gabled house,
the gambrel barn, papa's prize ram, even
Elijah our best herd dog come back to life.

Our etched-upon fungus placed attractively
among cousin's other wedding gifts.

Typus Orbis Terrarum*
*Lucy Thompson, Second Wife
of Rev. Jason Lee, October 1839*

Between bouts of seasickness,
I study Chinook jargon: Your heart good,
you go to God. Make *hyack*.
A force great within me
to win every soul in the crusade
against Satan's Empire. Father's clients,
the wealthy devout, loosened
their purse strings allowing each wave
to rap The Word against the good ship *Lausanne*
as she navigates New York Harbor—
tide in our favor, sails tightly furled.

My life, a dream: from Newberry Seminary—
those gray loaves of Vermont granite—to Oregon,
where the sun sets like a citrus into the sea.
A land, Husband says, so wood-thick,
the odor of resin overpowering. By night:
foreign stars white as the porcelain plates
I forsook as wedding gifts.
The heathen, Husband tells me, frightened
that praying will offend the salmon. Worse,
when a savage prays, he demands payment!
Husband confounded by the copperskins—
their disinterest, their many tongues.
Can't they see, he asks me,
their smallpox divinely sanctioned?

Ship rattle and beam moan, all passengers
ordered below. A southwest gale unfetters
the boom as waves assault our starboard. Sailing
backward, icebergs larger than barns
bring terror—even to Christians. Then,
becalmed waters: sailors mend jib sheets, shots
fired to chase gulls from riggings, and
my body suddenly delivered
of mal de mers misery. I ponder it:

When we lose sight of the eastern seaboard, will I
lose courage? I pray that my heart,
no longer landlocked,
will sail free around Cape Horn.

At the Captain's table, Husband traces
our voyage across water-stained charts.

Above green and aquatint, undulant clouds;
below—I cannot help but stare—a cartouche
quoting not our Savior, but Cicero. Soundings
and rhumb lines guide us through plagues
of sea dragons to *terra obscura,* north
of California Island.

Reverend Lee's mission-colony
shall remove forever our doomed copper brethren
from Britain's corrupting force. With ever-
increasing converts—mostly orphans,
mostly sick with chills— I will,
I must, be productive of good
in the amalgamation of savage blood,
instructing red wives in The Truth…otherwise,
they are but concubines. Their migratory habits,
their degraded behavior—so much to be done.
So many sinking into the grave,
a Happy Death their only hope: Accept Christ,
the Reverend begs, and live
in Heaven. But they understand not
scrofula and ague's root—their own
inherited evil. My job
keeper of the school ledger:
Labor credits in this column;
board, clothing, coffins in the other.

I study Chinook jargon: Good heart,
go to God. Make *hyack.*
My duty to dispense the Gospel
so all may die in Christ. Mindful
of my own health, Husband warns, a shadow
crossing his face. His first wife buried
with her infant in the Willamette grove

Jason Lee, 1803–45.

where she was wed. Now
in the ship's hold, her white
engraved headstone the marble ballast
upon which my hope chest rests:

Lo! We have left all, and followed thee.

* "Images of the World," drawn by Dutch cartographer
Abraham Ortelius (1527–1598)

A Mighty Fortress Is Our God

And though this world, with devils filled, should threaten to undo us;
We will not fear, for God hath willed His truth to triumph through us.

—Martin Luther, 1529

Considering Her Answer to a Letter[*]
Sent By Emigrant, Addressed:
"Catherine Sager, Somewhere in Oregon"
Catherine Sager Pringle, age 19,
December 21, 1854, Salem, Oregon Territory

Uncle,
the feathery leaves of the news of you
—posted last year—sit in my lap
like a tropical bird. Herein I enclose
a lock of my hair, a lock from each
of my three surviving sisters.
Uncle, have we cousins?
When and where were our parents born?
Do you know Ma's name
before she married?
If you have it, could you send
Grandfather's daguerreotype
for display at Matilda's wedding?
Could you send a knot of our mother's hair?
We long to know what our kin looked like.

Four of us remain.
I am married with a baby daughter.
Elizabeth teaches school and is engaged.
Matilda, age fifteen, will soon wed
a man of thirty—in Oregon
this is not unheard of; little Henrietta,
born near Scotts Bluff,
lives with me as does Elizabeth
who will write to you
as she may remember
more than I.

What do I recall of 1844?

The day we crossed the Platte;
inside our wagon at noon, hot
as a Dutch oven with its lid tight on

and not a single Chinese fan to be had.
I owned two dresses, wore
the cornflower blue for the love
of its added onto befurbelowed skirt.
Jumping from high places cooled me.
If I twirled, blue surrounded me with
a soothing skirt wind.

As I leapt from the moving wagon,
my ruffle caught the elbow
of an axe handle pulling me under,
the fore wheels pressing like
a shirt iron over my leg, the small
of my blue back.
Mother beseeched the sky with prayers.
Raw language shot from Father's mouth,
itself a wound, open and gaping.

Mother beseeched the sky again
when Father took high fever
after chasing buffalo on a day
hot enough to bake bread. The rattle
of those beasts' interlocked horns
heard for miles. At night sometimes
I still feel the heat of their sour breath.
They buried Father
at Green River. Mother,
left with a helpless older daughter,
newborn Henrietta, three other girls
under the age of eight,
two sons: ten and twelve.
Her sorrow, her feeble health, plus
the perplexities of travel
laid her beside the trail
after crossing Willow Creek.
Soon, everyone supposed,
I'd be buried beside the Powder.

But just after our bloodshod oxen
traversed the Blue Mountains, I rose,
stood, and with limp and cane walked
through disagreeably cold rain

Catherine Sager.

up to Dr. Whitman's mission.
His wife and he rejoiced at being counted
worthy to carry salvation's
glad tidings to the West and
the whole seven of us children taken in.
The next morning, our breakfast:
fresh bread spread with molasses.

We heard from emigrants who came
the year following: Henry Sager's grave
robbed, his bones left to bleach.

Naomi, our mother, dug up by wolves.
Out the Mission's kitchen window,
the pleasant view
of the Whitman baby's garden grave,
a comfort to her parents until
Providence ordained we be orphaned again.

I put aside the memory of the murder
of my guardians, both brothers,
the death of our petted sister Hannah
from measles. With my older brothers
died our history. Uncle,
the lives of your four nieces
from then until now
makes dull commentary, except

to say: a long tiresome trip
from the States to this country;
start as soon as the waterless sea of grass permits.
You cannot be too particular in your choice
of a sturdy Yankee schooner.
Wear canvas clothing or sage will strip you
and is hard on livestock.
Wild game uncertain, let your main load
be flour and bacon; your tool chest, of course;
clothes and bedding; your Bible, books—
histories of Greece and Rome. Put on three
good yoke of oxen; an extra pair
in case of lameness or sore neck.
Bring every loose cow

you can entice to follow.
When we left, all of us children sick and
continued so until the high desert when,
despite misfortunes like unabated rain,
we began to mend. Bless you, Uncle,
your answers bring the uncertain coastline
of our parents' lives closer to our harbor.
From here we send you our imperishable love
and our plain, well-beaten path.

In 1853, Frederick Sager of Iowa read a letter published in the Christian Advocate *concerning an orphan girl named Catherine Sager who had been taken into the home of a reverend in Salem, Oregon Territory. Frederick Sager remembered that his brother Henry, whom he hadn't heard from in ten years, had a daughter of that name.*

Matilda Jane Sager and her first husband, Lewis Hazlitt, 1855.

Henrietta Sager shortly before her death by accidental gunshot.

While Preparing to Ride to a Cayuse Village of New Converts Inundated by Measles, Dr. Marcus Whitman Inventories His Pack Horse's Bags While Considering: Which Sermon, Which Psalms, Which Prayers; *near Ft. Walla Walla, Oregon Country, November 1847*

listening trumpet
bloodletting lancets
glass mortar and pestle
dental pliers with various claws
tweezers
tracheotomy tube
bullet forceps
birthing forceps
sea sponge
cauterizing iron
tourniquet
trephine
trepanning brush
probe
horsehair sutures
quills
sharpening stone
tongs
3 candles
small apothecary scales
pewter syringe
small funnel
12 phials
12 gallipots
2 scalpels
physic spoon
sticking plaster
2 blankets

flannel
tow
lint

5 lumps myrrh
Peruvian fever bark
angostura bitters
ipecac
mustard
brimstone
tar ointment
mercurial ointment
aethiops mineral
castor oil
asafetida
whiskey
salt
vinegar
camphorated oil
aconite
Artemisia
bitter ash
essence of antimony
emetic tartar
cayenne pepper
Epsom salts
nitrite salt
liquid laudanum

rhubarb powder
Goulard's extract of lead
iron filings
turpentine
verdigris
ginger powder
contrayerva root
hogslard
basilicom unguent
white vitriol
opium
calomel
magnesia powder

Booklet: *Detecting by Percussion
Hidden Diseases in the Chest*

Vol. III, *The Cyclopaedia of Practical
Medicine: Comprising Treatises on
the Nature and Treatment of Diseas-
es, Materia Medica and Therapeutics,
Medical Jurisprudence, Etc., Etc.* by
Sir John Forbes

Bible, black leather bound, 15" x
10", bookmarked and annotated by
Narcissa Prentiss Whitman: Psalm
139 & John 14:
*Let not your heart be troubled: ye be-
lieve in God, believe also in me.
In my Father's house are many man-
sions: if it were not so, I would have
told you. I go to prepare a place for you.*

Lament of the Slatted Sunbonnets
Kate Thomas (b. 1841)

Picture a hundred wagons,
a kaleidoscope of people, some Godless
others refusing to travel on a Sunday,
women with care-worn faces, babies with fits,
twenty young chaps hired
to pilot the family's second schooner.
Nothing like it ever again in your life or mine.

i.

I was ten, my oldest brother
drove the stock. My friends and I
stayed out from underfoot; our mothers
knew us from afar by the color
of our slatted sunbonnets:
iris root gray, burdock, tan oak—
my bonnet dyed a flat sumac black.
One chum—something ferrety
about her face—had headgear
the immodest shade of flame—
surely Papists, Mother said.
Mornings, Father checked the horses' backs
for soreness, then yoked our oxen;
we girls scattered shiftless as grasshoppers.
Washday Monday discarded; the less said
about ironing the better. Every sunrise
brought a changeable wonder—
a clean sky flecked with clouds above the flat
silvery Platte, a mile wide at times.
We could not swim, nor could our parents,
but the oxen, born to it—heads high, necks
out of water. Why learn when nothing
could save man or beast from quicksand.

ii.

On we trudged across treeless
landscapes extending beyond
umbrella-shaped rocks that towered

a hundred feet above occasional beggar Indians
bedecked in feathers, trinkets, beads.
One fell away, another followed.
Our bloodleap quickened as we imagined
the secrets of their race.

Before sundown, the essentials—
wood, grass, wholesome water—secured,
our wagons halted. If a creek flowed by
we washed, holding fast
to our bonnets' balsa slats
and careful where we hung
our pantelettes; Indians might swipe them.
At night, always a fire
where we sang as one, "Good-bye Susannah";
a swing about its melody that caught
our fancy, the rhythm and pitch
of older girls' chiming voices
as they sparked with Steve, our favorite
hired driver. Hair the color
of Mother's best biscuits, he knew sleights
of hand, could mesmerize people—some people,
my brother, sometimes. One night,
wrapped in blankets, he pretended to be Sioux.
When he scared our mothers witless,
the sunbonnets fell prostrate;
our immoderate laughter severely scolded.
Father never doubted Oregon
would make him rich, Mother happy;
that in five years we'd return to Ohio to visit,
a given. We rose again at the cymbal clash
of a new sun's yellow noise.

                    iii.
No one cared that the sunbonnets rode
astride mule or horse. Sometimes I'd try
to stand in the saddle to catch Steve's eye—
I mightn't have perfect pitch, but
I had perfect balance. Steve lectured
(mostly to Little Miss Flame Bonnet):
The humpback buffalo has a donkey tail
that, when he makes a pie, coils

into a script unclosed "O."
Soon bison chips our mainstay;
we spoke mostly of Steve while gathering
sun-baked cakes that burned like straw.

When rag-and-bone Cheyennes appeared
bearing strings of trout, Steve bartered
shiny bits: a penny, a fork with bent tines.
He spoke to them with wild gesticulations.
Chinook jargon, a tongue so full
of pops and clicks crumbling into our peals
of laughter, we were sure
it was a chewed up language he'd invented.

                    iv.
We ate buffalo, which was coarse,
and pronghorn antelope
tasting like stovetop pigeon.
From tartar and trail alkali,
Mother made delicious cream soda;
primitive ice cream from South Pass's
dazzling snow—treats to distract us
from so many despoiled roadside graves.
When we supped on dried cod and wild peas
for meals on end, it was the Lord doing for us
what He'd done for the Israelites. Still
after crossing Little Sandy, some deserted
at the cutoff to Sacramento.

We forged a narrow river
named for its grassy color. Two days
west of Fort Hall a half-breed scout
warned us of warring hostiles. Our fathers
regretted trading with Natives,
rifles for buffalo robes, but
we saw not one Crow or Blackfoot.
When we halted for lunch beside the music
of Rock Creek, a Snake chief appeared,
his face and arms a tapestry. Steve bartered:
How much for Miss Flame Bonnet?
When the chief offered ten ponies,
we cut up in laughter. They haggled.

Fifteen. What skylarking.
Twenty horses. Sold!
After Steve traded my chum, I cried:
Why hadn't he bartered me?
The Indian went away. We rolled on
over what is now Idaho.
When I whined, Steve consoled:
obviously savages favored red.

Next forenoon, the chief discharged
a score of spotted Cayuses loose
with our stock, demanding his wife.
Steve explained: Whites don't trade for women.
Not seeing the joke, the chief turned angry
and exacting; our Wagon Captain sent him away.
That night, no moon, only warm calm,
cascades of stars, sometimes a coyote complained.
We didn't hear dusky figures creep up
until our livestock stampeded.
Mother shrieked, wrung her hands, called
on God. A party of menfolk followed—
one badly injured by poison-tipped
obsidian arrow; they turned back.
After the excitement, the sun bonnets—
Flame, Sumac Black, Iris Root,
Burdock, Tan Oak—fell asleep
exhausted from mingling tears
and prayers and sightings of Steve.

Come crimson-skied dawn, Father found
not one mule or ox or horse. Fifty
of our one hundred wagons abandoned.
Flame Bonnet's father swore
to kill Steve. Mother cried to leave
towels, quilts, monogrammed tablecloths
she'd woven by hand. I cringed:
the only item saved from our schooner,
a six-pound flat iron; a wedding gift
from Grandmum—not what I'd have chosen.

The court of our fathers passed sentence:
Steve banished;

if he tried to return, he'd be shot.
The forsaken wagons set ablaze
to save them from Indians—a pyre
of grass and trees that almost consumed
our few remaining oxen.
Each sunbonnet gave Steve her lunch,
his only provisions. We watched him
for the last time as he lit out,
cornbread hair blowing, walking
toward the southwest where hostiles
with reptilian patience hid
in rock crevices, greasewood,
behind shifting mounds of sand.
Let death be swift, we prayed.
Our fathers forbade him forever
the Willamette Valley. We cried:
without Steve we were dancers
with no one to call the quadrille.

v.

Age ten and older had to walk;
we sunbonnets trudged
for two months choked by dust.
After a week, our shoes and stockings
wore out, we stumbled barefoot in shale
to the clank-thud of our discordant voices
and the clank-thud of our troubled hearts.
We no longer feared death, but
looked forward to the Resurrection,
which we hoped would happen soon.

What came were Indians
in gaudy finery riding fleet ponies.
Bacon, coffee, flour, more
than one beef cow demanded
as rent for the grass our few cattle ate.
We soon ran out of food and fished
the serpent river's devious water.
Then an even harder pull
over hilly sage and lava into the Blue
Mountains traversed in snow and
blemished by black-crusted blueberries—at least

for now we wouldn't starve. But
our oxen footsore, famished, our one wagon
shaved and whittled down, our last
feather mattress, Mother's English china
left disconsolately on the trail.
When soldiers from The Dalles
brought us four pounds flour each,
the sun bonnets choked on dough
before bread could be baked.

vi.

I can't hope to explain our happiness
when we arrived. Instead of striking off
each morning, walking stub-toe
barefoot through cactus and snakes,
we stepped into grass belly-deep
on our frail cattle; sea breezes
billowing what looked like sails
of changeable green silk.

vii.

For my thirteenth birthday,
I received a spinning wheel
and shares of wool to dye and spin.
Flame bonnet's father
picked out her husband, a neighbor
who'd claimed one square section
and now with a wife could claim another.
My oldest brother married Iris Gray
and when she died he went with
my husband (picked him out myself—
a biscuit-haired Blacksmith)
to mine Idaho's Orofino.
War in the States, no dry goods,
no legal tender to buy them with even if
they could be had. A bitter November,
deep-crusted snow, my husband
turned back. My brother lost
his money and his way. Knocking
on a dugout's leather-hinged door,
a man answered, asked:
Would your name be Thomas?

I crossed the plains with you, he said,
at least part of the way—Steve.
My brother dumbfounded,
his life saved by a man our father
would have shot—had, instead, kept
to cover, avoided hostiles,
taken in by a train to California
where he'd mined and prospered.

Steve gave my brother work
scratching out enough glitter
to pay our parents' way
back to Ohio before they died.
One brittle night in front of the fire,
my brother reminisced:
For years you were the music
of my sister's thoughts—each
small pleasure endlessly recounted.
Steve's face a puzzle:

You had a sister?

Wagons crossing a river.

Every Stormy Wind That Blows

There is a place where Jesus sheds
The oil of gladness on our heads;
From every stormy wind that blows,
From every swelling tide of woes,
There is a calm, a sure retreat;
'Tis found beneath the mercy seat.

—Hugh Stowell, 1831

Cloth

Elizabeth Millar Wilson (b. 1830), The Dalles, Oregon

First of March, winter's chill
made me desirous of work.
Just as I graduated Troy Seminary,
a call from Oregon for teachers:
homes promised, situations assured,
all steamer expenses paid.
It was a plunge into the bleak
off New York dock.
With satchels of primers, *Harper's Monthly*,
and *Ladies Indispensable Assistant*, I dove
sailing to palm-and-papyrus shores of winter unknown,
reading to pass the hours:

In cashmere haloed by Cantonese crepe,
Drapery gives grace to the statuesque bride

When I went off to school,
Mother'd given me my first subscription—
those magazines, my life rafts,
I saved them for years.

At the Isthmus, we were towed
up the Chagres by a broken-down steamer,
at Gatun, sequestered in a hut,
sixteen of us to a small room.
I must have appeared a monster
to native women, I stood much the taller;
they wore only white, cooked us scorched corn.
Pocked by mosquitoes, I spent the night
in safety, but not in slumber. Next eve
slept onboard atop trunks which paved the hull.
At Gorgona, the American Hotel,
two rooms, new cots, sheets, slips
on each pillow. I wanted to stay forever.

A piece of Valenciennes lace at the throat,
The skirt flounces: a cloud of overlapping pongee

The next day my sidesaddle strapped to a mule
for transit to the hill where Balboa
first saw the South Sea. Finally
the walls of Panama City, forty feet high,
wide as horse-and-cart, crowned with watchtowers.
Quartered in a vast apartment spread thick with cots,
I was detained for weeks.

Pale complexions necessitate bonnets lined in pink silk,
Long sashes fastened in front preferable to belts

In the marketplace I bought oranges, a dress pattern
of the sheerest white muslin ever seen, soft
as rabbit, plus watered velvet ribbon.
I'd no groom in mind, but surely someday
I'd change my name and would need...

A fine dress of white peau de soie low on the shoulders,
A demi basque before and behind

We sailed for California, coaled at Acapulco
taken ashore on the shoulders of natives.
A shaft broke, we went on one wheel,
two died at sea. We saw on shore volcanic fires,
stopped at the port of Mazatlan, then
a forest of ships' masts called San Francisco.

Ivory alpaca loose across the chest,
Sleeves sans trimmings becoming to full figures

If this advice useless to me, surely
a friend would find it handy. I caressed
the pages with only gloved hands.

There wasn't a dock. We anchored, went ashore
in lifeboats. That night I got no sleep
due to callers, more money offered
to teach than ever I earned in Oregon.
Temptations to digress everywhere, but

At the waist, a frill of embroidered nansouk,
Narrow tatting at the wrist gives finish to a dress

the next day found me aboard the *Columbia*
bound for a river of that name,
the region of eternal summer traded
for a gray coast spotted with driftwood camps.
At Portland, I walked the gangplank
through a double line of gazers,
the entire population, never seeing women.
This one-sided community in the end decided
I'd too much experience,
the crowd objecting that a limit
ought to have been set,
no teacher accepted out of her teens!
As I traversed seas of mud to a whaler
bound up stream, they voted me, at twenty-one,
too long in the tooth. Our boatman,
under the influence of whisky,
stranded us on a bar. No supper, no wrap,
never a worse night in my life, so I thought.

Hair arranged in bandeaux, half-puffed at the sides,
Netted in taffeta, ornamented by blossoms

The next issue months in the mail,
arriving with pages well-thumbed.

The following morning, by horse
to where I was engaged to teach.
The first ten miles endured—I had never
ridden except by Isthmusian mule—
the next ten, torture. I'd no longer
misgivings or fears or presentiments,
but lived by the minute, not allowed to dismount
even when I gave my word I wouldn't lie down;
the last ten miles I have no words for
except: Mules forever for me.
I hadn't the energy to speak for days.

At my assigned school simplicity ruled:
in unseasonable heat
not one Chinese fan, but twigs
bent round, both ends hand held,
a kerchief over the whole.

My worst trouble not with teaching grammar,
but visitors: men, curious, unsympathetic,
rode for days, striding into my schoolroom
to await the hour of dismissal.
The giggles of older girls,
no amount of clothing
could shield me from their knowing looks,
their whispers: *Teacher's got a beau.*
I burned with mortification. Nothing
learned at seminary prepared me
and no hint of advice in *Harper's*
or *Ladies Assistant.* All the same,
alone in my room after hours,
I climbed between their covers
and with a page held in each hand
like oars, I rowed until late, knowing
that nothing could change
the cloth from which I had been cut.

Portland, First and Stark Streets, 1852.

The Doll

Marianne Hunsaker Edwards D'Arcy (b. 1842),
Oregon City

Due to secret dread,
I was an old maid; my friends long wed
before I married at nineteen.
As a tyke, nuns taught me to pray
and when I got mountain fever
I prayed for death. Papa thought
I would not recover and dug my grave.
But I could not bear to die
as I would never see Mother again.

At age six, Father arranged to put me
in the Sisters of Notre Dame school
while he and mother and the babies
went to mill lumber on the Washougal.
I bled tears into my pillow each night
after one of the older girls told me
most students were orphans.
I had no idea what that meant.
Their parents had died, she said,
or gone to the gold fields. Obviously
I had been given away to nuns.

I felt panic, sorry I hadn't died of fever. Worse
Sister Mary Louise introduced me
as her new girl, proof of my abandonment.
I cried all the time and had to be led away
to contemplate my sins, the greatest of which
as near as I could determine
was not dying with my brother and sister
after Father had gone to all the hard work
of digging my grave. To cheer me,
Sister brought a nibble of gingerbread
which I thought the food of heaven.

Sunday evenings, we gathered
in the high-ceilinged dining hall.

Here we were allowed our treasures:
bits of gold and silver paper, shapes
of broken china, a scrap of lace. We'd never
seen a doll. A new girl arrived
from Sacramento, her eyes
the color of tea. When she unwrapped
her treasure, I stood speechless,
so wrought up, my heart kicked.
Would Sister Mary Louise strike me
for loving a doll more than God?
I felt Gabriel's wings beat a hot wind
above my head. I'd never been in love.
The new girl rewrapped her toy
in a piece of sunburst gingham
the same color as Mother's best dress.

Could I hold Pretty? I asked,
taking the dolly to a corner, memorizing
her coin-sized face, the opal eyes and nub
of a nose. I'd never seen such loveliness.
Then, as if Satan grabbed my arm,
I thrust Pretty to my mouth. Jabbing
her head between my lips, I bit:
the crunch of plaster, shards cutting my tongue.
Paralyzed with fright and guilt, what
would be done to me; would I go to prison?
I wrapped up the doll, returning it to the girl.
Thank you, I said in a voice not my own.

That night the noise of my heart shook the bed,
wolves screamed terrible vowels,
the wind a clatter of irate consonants.
I wanted my mother. I wanted to hide my face
in the skirt of her sunburst gingham dress.

I had one friend, just a tot with hair
like birch curlings. The next morning
Sister Mary Louise gave me an extra spoonful
of blood pudding and said that Jesus
had taken her in the night.

Monday passed, Tuesday, Wednesday evening;
when would the jailer come for me?
A week went by, another. Finally I inquired:
What about your doll?
Don't you know? the new girl said, rats
chewed off Pretty's face. The dread

that I'd be found out with me for years.
The grave father dug for me, what did it say
that it had never been filled in? So often terror
visited me: if ever I married, mightn't I
savage my own innocent babe?

The Stove

Martha Gay Masterson Remembers
October 28, 1852
Eugene, Oregon Territory

The groom arrived late, likewise the parson.
No organ, the wedding march a steady patter
of rain with a trumpet fanfare of migrating geese.
From a side door, the bridal party entered.
Father could not bear to watch—Mamie
had always been his pet. Holding baby Pink close,
he paced the dooryard. And I?
Always had Sissy with me; no one else for a friend.
How would I live without her?
Nine brothers. Pink, age eighteen months,
was born on the trail—that frayed

Ribbon of suffocating dust.
The first thing Mamie and I did when camped—
scamper off, always better able
to battle snakes by clinging to one another.
If we found graves, we'd read their inscriptions.
If wolves had broken in
we'd look for the ropey yellow braids
of young girls like ourselves.
At first we shunned the skulls—sun and storm
blemished, scattered everywhere. Finally
we picked one up, another, reading verses
passersby had inscribed across the brainpan.
Adding a line or two of our own, we'd place each
to attract other emigrants to our handiwork, then
move on: father, mother, twelve children,
one daughter-in-law, and our Missouri neighbor.

September, we crossed the Deschutes,
Barlow's Gate, climbed the Cascades in rain-
storm footing over rocks, fallen trees—
our party so slow others pleaded to pass us by.
The tattered oxen fell, rose, fell to rise no more;
everything we could do without cast aside.

At Zigzag Creek, Mamie and I fished
with pin hooks and thread lines.
It was my idea to investigate
the old left-behind stove—
six burners, a rampart of black curlicues.
As sister placed the toe of her size-four shoe
on the iron hearth, a drover came up
and spoke to her. Another joined in.
When they rode away, we heard the first man say:
"That sloe-eyed girl? I'm going to marry her."
We giggled. He hadn't asked her name.
His hair a curly smokestack kin to the stove.

A year later we'd a temporary kitchen—
four posts supporting a roof; our furniture
the wagon boxes where we slept
off the ground safe from snakes.
I'd just washed up, hung all cups
and milking buckets from the makeshift eaves.
The men gone back to mowing when
a stranger with a steel wool beard rode in.
Mamie? He asked, tying his horse to a kitchen post.
The horse had whims of his own, snapped his teeth,
and seeing a scarecrow where there wasn't one,
shied, pulling down our kitchen.

Father finished our fireplace and
five-room log house just as Oregon's
equinoctial rains began. *The Day* rolled around.

Groomsman, preacher, neighbors filled
the whole of our new first floor.
The ceremony short,
Mamie's happiness sealed. Afterward
at the wedding supper I told
of their first meeting at the old stove,
our new rafters ringing when I said:
that afternoon by the Zigzag—
we thought we'd caught no fish. As sister
left on horseback, I threw a slipper after her
for luck. The wedding march beating
against our roof brought me no comfort.

We'd not yet planted the stone orchard
on the hill behind home. Mamie's daughters
the first to rest there; Pink would follow.
Though father often warned: life is filled
with sunshine and shadow,
none of us had learned this then.

John Cogswell and Mary Frances (Mamie) Gay on their wedding day, October 28, 1852.

Brother Churchianity's Garden
Matilda Sager Delaney (b. 1839)

As a child I was taught: *forgive,*
but nowhere does the Bible say
I have to forget the wholesome truth.

After my parents died
of mountain fever, after
my brothers and my guardians
were murdered, after Peter Skene Ogden
bought us from the Indians,
I was taken to Forest Grove
into the one-room lean-to home
of an intensely religious preacher.

If the fireplace coals died overnight, I walked
barefoot and bare legged over frost
to the neighbors for a shovelful.
An eight-year-old child cannot forget
Brother Churchianity's wife pacing the floor
with a toothache cured
by knockout with a steel punch
used for mending harness leather.

As he saddled up, my new guardian instructed:
cut a switch thick as my thumb.
I found a good one, for his horse, I thought,
poor beast. I'd need correction
while he was gone, he said, flogging
my backside, then promised to beat me again
when he got back. For years I wore
the violets-and-stems bouquet
of bruises and welts. Whipped so often
it grew on me like Oregon rain:
cold and inevitable, to be borne without complaint.
My body a garden harrowed by coach whip,
quirt, cane, belt, bridle strap.
To this day I cannot look upon
a deeply red red rose.

Brother Churchianity left
no feed for his sheep,
which froze or were eaten by wolves.
My job to pull wool from lamb carcasses,
washing away feces and grease in the icy creek.
His wife carded and spun, knitting socks
sold to miners else we'd have starved.

When Reverend returned,
he told me to fetch my bonnet,
catch his horse, climb up behind.
We rode all day to a crowd assembled
beneath a hardwood maple. My guardian said
he wanted to impress upon me
what happens when a child does not mind
her elders. The sheriff brought out a man
and hanged him. I still had nightmares
about the death of my brothers by hatchet blade.
For months I woke up frozen
in sweat, dreaming of the executed:
eyes popped, protruding tongue,
the way he twitched.

I was beaten for going to a theatrical
at the Congregational church
where I met Lewis Hazlitt twice my age;
I was whipped for befriending Mary Allen,
a girl born out of wedlock.
Finally the neighbors complained.
I testified in court.
Brother Churchianity pleaded
with the hanging Judge:
If I was bound out to him,
he could fully control me. After
they argued, I mounted my own defense

And married Lewis Hazlitt on his way
to the gold fields. I won't say
we had a good life, but we had five children.
When Mr. Hazlitt died, I had to take in wash.
Today, I've outlived three husbands. No man
ever worked me as hard as that clergyman.

When people tell me I'm vindictive,
I want to ask: of the flowers in your garden,
how deeply red the rose? When you consider
lilies of the field, do you see the white
unblemished backsides of children?
Do you ever notice how willingly
the necks of spring flowers bend
beneath the battering of an April rain?

Well, answer me, do you?

Matilda Jane Sager and Lewis Mackey Hazlitt, 1855.

The surviving Sager sisters, Catherine, Elizabeth, Matilda, later in life.

An Answer For Mr. Anderson

Sarah Jane Sturgess, age 13 ½, 1851,
near Ft. Vancouver, Oregon Territory

All day our neighbor's hired man
bends hazelwood into barrel hoops.
At night he visits for the comfort
of my molasses-colored hair.
You have a swan neck, he tells me.
Then you may call me Swan, I say.
It's best, he says, to name children
after generals to give them courage. What
about the girls? I ask. We play this game:
When I close my eyes, what do I see?

It's always the same: the afternoon I lost
the only doll I ever owned, I see Father
swimming our cattle across the Snake.
He slips off his horse; the burning
turpentine smell of greasewood
fills my lungs. I watch Mother's face,
her blush— Father's favorite rose—turns
fog-colored, her eyes sink like valleys
below the peaks of cheekbones sharper
than the Blue Mountains ahead of us.
I see Father's hat, a bird's nest, floating
downstream. Father's dark hair
disappears, bobs up; one hand,
fingers sharp as an axe, chops
the surface as he strokes after the horse, but
the red roan swims faster and
Father's head drops
through a calm floor of water
reflecting the pure
white of one cloud and branches
of Gilead trees along shore—nothing speaks
of the suck in the river
that ate two men that day.

I miss Father, I used to miss Dolly, but never
mention to Mr. Anderson how heavy
my little crosses. What to do
with the clothes I made for her?
During months of widowhood,
Mother traded with an Indian
Father's shirts for fish. Tonight
I report: half a morning's walk
to the Hudson Bay store
from Coal Creek where I speak
Chinook so often, I mistake it
for English. Today Mother and I bought
light-colored Shanghai silk
in a window-pane pattern
after the proprietor showed us
magazine sketches
—Victoria's royal wedding—
then suggested: cuffed bell sleeves, a high
V-neck, the skirt gathered just above
the natural waist. When I close my eyes,

I tell Mr. Anderson: I see our daughter
wearing my wedding gown as she marries
on the porch of the house he will build
for us beside a hazelnut tree. In her hand,
a cup of moonlight: one unfurling bloom—
Father's climbing musk-scented rose
grown from a bare root that Mother
could not bring herself to trade away.

Sarah Jane Sturgess Anderson and William Reese Anderson, 1877.

That Long Looked-For Day

Elder Edgerton's Confidential Advice
to Courting Gentlemen,
Western Ontario, Canada, 1862

If sincerely fatigued by single-blessedness,
by cold untended fires, meals
burned or frostbitten or bland;
then best you learn
how to extract bliss from lovely lips.
Step one: eat no baked beans or biled pork.
Be on time.
As all persons—women especially—
are governed by first impressions and externals,
neatness better than richness, plainness
better than display. And remember
nothing deforms a man more
than a bad haircutting.
Don't itch. Don't eat raw onions.
Never pick your teeth, nose, scabs: spit
as little as possible, never on the floor.
Do you wonder what she's thinking?
   Of that piece of her sister's
   wedding cake she put beneath her pillow
   and dreamed of…who?
   Did he look like you?
The only thing you should scratch
is her history and never in mixed company.
Three times a bridesmaid?
Third or fourth engagement?
A desperate flirt? Perhaps,
or just another instance
of female inconsistency.

Upon rising Sunday morning:
wash profusely to avoid the itch
of ringworm—remove all crust, rub on
sublimate of mercury, spirits of wine,
tincture of musk. Never
neglect to perfume your breath.

Attend your own congregation first,
in the afternoon frequent her church, and
at evening go together to a third house of worship.
What's she thinking? Pleasant thoughts:
        a horseshoe of daisies, a white dress
        of oriental muslin, sprigs
        of orange blossom pinned at her neck.
Be cautious of taking her out
for a drive and getting lost or eating
pie together alone in her kitchen.
How to kiss? It's easy
though many fail.
First, know who. Second, don't jump
at her like a trout smacking her neck,
don't peck like a pigeon or drool
like a dog. Take her left hand
in your right, draw her toward you.
What's she thinking?
        Jelly tarts, raspberry preserves,
        Spanish buns, coffee and tea,
        followed by pears and grapes and wedding cake.
Lay her head on your shoulder.
You should be the taller so
stand to it, don't sit.
Don't knock off her hairpiece
or hat though it be several stories too tall.
What's she thinking?
        Auntie C—glass rolling pin,
        Grandmother—silver fruit basket,
        Lizzie and Marie—engraved teaspoons.
Take careful aim, don't be afraid
of the erect altar of love, kissing
doesn't hurt. And if you make
a mistake, if you miss
or kiss the wrong girl? Well,

Consider it the foot of providence
stepping in. You won't be
the first to flee to where
your troubled past is yet unknown.

"Verbena Tea and Dill Hinder the Witches of Their Will"
The Jottings of Granny Wintersteen, undated

If these don't work and
you find yourself with a houseful
of girls, too many stillborn,
or just too many,
there are other methods:
The seed of Queen Anne's lace
a teaspoon a day
not to be confused
with hemlock;
morning and night a cup
of rue broth or pennyroyal tea.

Half a cored lemon inserted up there
when he isn't looking;
sea sponges soaked in soap suds,
seed wool soaked in vinegar
with a daily chew of cotton root.

This recipe works for many:
When cool, cut like fudge
in half-inch squares,
use each time:
One pound cocoa butter,
one ounce boric acid,
tannin drawn from oak galls,
one and a half ounce; mix
melt over boiling water,
turn into a pie pan. It smells
good enough to eat and
will not harm or arouse

his suspicion.

Cynthia, Judge Stafford's First Wife
Auburn (Baker County), Oregon, March 24, 1863

I did not teach today. The pain
in my head makes my ears ring.
Six months here in Freezeout Gulch
amid stick figures of rattle-bone wormwood
known as sage. Pulling blankets
the color of fog up under my chin
a thread catches a crack in my lip.
My feet cold, but I cannot will these hands
to warm them. My gaze traces
S patterns in the bark of this rough-cut
log hut husband secured for us. I think
of his fingers—how I kissed each bruise—
sore from sluicing, repairing riffles. Reaching
across the bed for him: empty space. I remember

At Cedar Falls we married,
my teaching contract almost up. Cyrus:
childhood friend, ex-infantry man,
lawyer, an Episcopalian like me. Papa
did not entirely approve our plan:
trek to the Far West, scratch
the gold fields securing savings, then
back to Potsdam—a gentleman's farm amid kin.

Left Iowa May 9th; arrived October.
I walked for weeks, trekked until night
—30 miles—then walked
a little longer, never getting into a wagon.
I got no sympathy from anyone but my husband
and at the end of day, I cooked outdoors
for unprincipled families of twenty
who carried our goods which
in the end we lost. Here now in a place
you will not find on any map.
So prostrate I cannot hold a pen,
my health in tatters. After leaving school
at Mt. Holyoke, I wanted to teach in foreign lands
and indeed am in one, though not Palestine.

Auburn: This smoke-filled damp air
the shade and density of clotted wool.
The butcher shop, like most mercantiles,
located outdoors on a split-log-of-a-table-top.
I shall say no more, except
Main Street parallel to Blue Canyon Creek,
all other avenues catawampus.
This place never had an inhabitant
until last spring and now 5,000!
Stabbings, hangings—one man dragged to death
by mob—little observance of the Sabbath;
the only conversation: treasure and what
to trade for how much whiskey.

No windows with glass, no bedstead, not
one chair, my fire's warmth escapes
up the mud-n-stick chimney. I reach
for Cyrus across splintery boards nailed up
to sleep and eat on—then remember:
Gone forty days after bacon-potatoes-flour, back
before we're trapped by arctic ice 'til spring…
Now he's come and gone again
this time to Boise's brighter goldbars.
His absence cuts my soul like cankers
cut my mouth.
I did not teach today. The pain
in my head makes blizzards rise
and fall in my gut, all I can eat
is snow, which soothes the tongue but
the stomach rejects.

A knock? Who's there? I must
get out of bed, unlatch the door. Where's
my bonnet, my tortoise shell comb?
Up gulch, a congregation of miners
dig in the little boneyard next to a wall
of tailings piled by Chinamen—
all those resting places unmarked
except by brown snow-broken grass.
This fever's dark dreams: I see
Cyrus at midlife in crow-black judge's robes
standing on the steps of a turreted house;

a child runs across the lawn, presents him
a family album—its cover marbled gold
and blood. Husband passes it to me as if
handing down a verdict.
I search each page. Nowhere
on these parchment leaves do I find
myself, my likeness, my name,
not a whisper—*Cynthia*—not one
breath of me.

Cynthia Mirandia Abram Stafford.

Cyrus Stafford.

About These Trumpeters That Line My Walls

Elizabeth Shepard Holtgrieve (b. 1840)

Mother died in Iowa
the Christmas I was nine,
just before we went west.
Ten years after meeting Father,
my stepmother died. They first
saw each other near a Boise River switchback
when our wagon train joined hers.
Two days later, Father told Miss Nelson
they ought to take advantage
of a preacher being present
and get married. I remember
Miss Nelson bringing her things to our wagon,
we'd not much room to begin with.
I slept outside under the running gear,
awakening to…white foals swimming
in the backwater? No—
swans, the first I'd ever seen.
Just before Father's wedding, a little playmate
took fever and died. Another thing
I'm not likely to forget about that terrible
cholera summer of '52: a few miles east
of The Dalles we passed a wagon pulled
to the side of the road: Seven children
cowering inside. Their parents had died
and they didn't know what to do.
I'll always remember the polish in the little boy's
frightened nut-brown eyes. I tried to comfort him:
surely swans had taken his parents to heaven
along with my friend. When I got to know
Miss Nelson, I wanted to be like her.
Once, after we'd settled here on Columbia Slough,
Father cursed up a cyclone because
our boat commenced sinking and nobody'd
thought to bring a dipper. My stepmother
bailed water with her sunbonnet which saved us.

That little boy's eyes sweated
through my thoughts as I cut brush
clearing father's land.
Rafting to Portland to buy fruit trees,
we spent the night in the hut
of a boatman who had a friend in want
of a wife, a situation that pulled
up the tips of Father's down-turned
horseshoe-shaped mouth.
To my amazement, Father arranged it
so that this friend would come upriver to our place
in two weeks—his twenty-eighth birthday—
and we'd marry. I was fourteen.
Henry and I did our courting during the three
days it took to paddle to his claim.

At times the small lake on our place
blackened with ducks and geese.
Next minute I'd look up
from a colicky baby or doctoring a cow,
the pond a frothy white—great flocks
of wintering swans touched down here;
you can't imagine the noise. It even
affected the herd, their udders
tightened, we'd less milk to sell. Birds
the size of bateaux, vast wings flapping
like mainsails. Their bugling
caused so many unspeakable visions to fly
unbidden into my head—I thought
the Rapture had come.

Now, other than the likenesses
of white trumpeters framed on my walls,
I haven't seen a swan in years.
My daughters Oceana and Henrietta
married and moved away, Charlie
lives with me, Mary is dead, John farms
the old place. You would have heard
of Arianne—her drawings of swans here
look just like life—but she died young;
Ben farms our place out on the slough;

my eldest, Emma (some mistook us
for sisters) married Zachariah Fitzgerald—
you remember him, the boy
in the wagon on the side of the road
whose parents had died, the one with polish
in his nut-brown eyes.

Mrs. Darby, Third Cousin to a Royal Confectioner, Gives Advice on Baking a Wedding Cake Modeled after the Spire atop London's St. Bride's Church—

for Fifty Guests including Keepsakes, Spokane, Washington Territory, 1859

First, attend the fire,
making sure you've enough
wood to last through baking.
Second, gather: eighty eggs,
half the weight of eighty eggs
in flour, the weight of eighty eggs
in sugar, thirty tablespoons lemon juice
and filings of the grated rinds of five.

Beat yolks ten minutes, add sugar, beat
until thick, add lemon juice, rind,
sieve flour; cut and fold in
stiffly beaten whites. Pour
into ten greased tins—suet
less likely to burn than butter—bake.

Frost when cold while considering
a harmony of sugar carved, shaped, sculpted
columns supporting cupids, coats
of arms, bride and groom figurines
draped in Grecian garb, doves,
seraphim and cherubim.

For the filling: mix, cook while stirring
10 cups cream
10 tablespoons butter
20 eggs
10 cups sugar
20 tablespoons tarter
10 cups grated preserved coconut.

Or layer with whipped cream and jam.

For the frosting, mix, beat, spread:
10 cups sugar
10 egg whites
10 teaspoons rose water
5 teaspoons lemon juice.

As to embellishments, use the patterning
from the bride's best embroidery:
chain stitched borders, cockle shells,
ropes, scrolls, petals, leaves,
roses, Gerber daisies, hydrangeas,
dots, lace, candles, musical scores,
lattice, fleur de lis, chrysanthemums.
Always, always, always basket-weave
the sides of the bottom tier.

Happy is a bride when the sun shines, but
when rain threatens, the sight
of a spired cake trimmed in orange
blossoms twined with myrtle
will steady her resolve.

The Brides of Christ Consider the Hunger of 100 Children, the 40 Sick, and Many Old Men Who Linger without Relative or Memory

Mother Joseph of the Sacred Heart*
to Sister Mary of the Precious Blood,
Mission of the Sisters of Providence,
Ft. Vancouver, Washington Territory, 1864

Sister, we cannot dwell on the drudgery
of these begging tours, our grim need
for money and our desperate straits.
To you, of the Precious Blood, God gave
the face of a dogwood flower,
one that pries handouts from the tight-fisted
without ever a "no" lodged in the heart.
Et por moi, God had another plan:
men hear in me the abrasive bugle
of a water buffalo while from your lips,
Sister Mary Precious, the words
of this impossible *Anglais* pour like mead.

Nearly ten years here and the language
still confounds me, as do the Americans
and their mysterious paper money.
No matter who translates,
our convent abacus screams *debit,*
debt, credit denied, along with one other
important truth: Now is the time
to acquire land, to celebrate
our belief in mortar and stone,
to build and build impressively because
what we erect upholds the Glory of God.
Each day the number of sufferers
and the price of real estate escalate.
Sister, with your seraph's face framed
in crisp bandeaux and the veil
of one who is fully professed, go

to the garrison Commander, beg
for the lumber from his torn-down fort.
Tonight I will point out the timbers I covet,
the best oak beam and ironwood lintel.

If I went to the Colonel, my jaw would trip
over his indecipherable verbs. I swear
on my carriage-maker father's grave
I can read every timber from ash to zebrawood,
I have heard every confession a saw can exact.
Trust me, my Sister, I know which beam
black-hearted or faithful; unmistakable
the scent of well-seasoned close-knit oak.
A tree, Sister Mary, is like a good Christian,
the toughest birch tempered by storm,
bent by wind, supple enough to endure;
no sapling sheltered from winter's pain
will make good lumber.
Think of it: a foundling home, a hospital—
a celestial chariot for each of us. Sister,
I place my father's toolbox before you,
so that you may venerate the haft
of this pale brown elmwood axe.

I was weaned on wood and the blood
of tools. Even in sleep I know how to grasp
the hickory handle of a hammer to best advantage.
I love the power it brings me almost as much
as I love God. See, I keep it close,
hooked here on my belt. With this,
and a saw, chisel, draw-knife, square,
let us build a Holy House;
let us feel the sudden expansive joy
of our vocation swirl in our hearts
till we can scarcely breathe
for the happiness in us. Does it matter
whose army governs this land or
that our store of silver is small
and our English pitiful?

We have come here to lay up treasure
for our True Home. Imagine it:

hearths for fires, walls for crucifixes.
When the chapel bell tolls six slow knells,
the wind of our chariot will fan the flames
of altar candles enkindling evergreens.
Follow me now while I taste the blazing
incense cedar and resinous pine; together
our eyes will close, our souls depart, and
our Bridegroom cometh. Neither God
nor words can fail us, my sister,
for the language of suffering
needs no interpreter.

Esther Pariseau (b. 1823), St. Elzear, Quebec

The five foundresses of the Sisters of Providence Northwest Mission in Oregon Territory. Seated (from left): Praxedes of Providence, Mother Joseph of the Sacred Heart, Mary of the Precious Blood. Standing (from left): Vincent de Paul, Blandine of the Holy Angels.

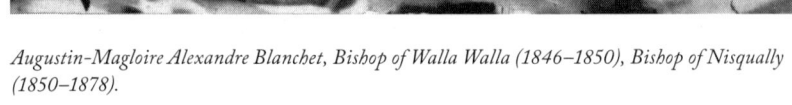

Augustin-Magloire Alexandre Blanchet, Bishop of Walla Walla (1846–1850), Bishop of Nisqually (1850–1878).

The Widow: Her Song
without Words sans Piano

Elizabeth Paschal Dillon Gay (b. 1838)

You have no idea of my difficulties.
Father died on the battlefield, Brother
joined the Union Army a few days after
I married Dr. Dillon.
The winter of '62 we walked
most of the way, Ohio to Oregon,
gave a ten dollar gold piece so our baby girl
could ride in someone's hickory wagon.
I sang lullabies, marching songs,
the only way baby wouldn't cry—
so tired sometimes it did not seem
I could take another step.

In Blue Canyon I took in wash,
melting snow over an open fire,
a brass kettle my only helpmate. Husband
a top surgeon when sober, but
tradesmen's wives subtracted money owed
to my laundry business
and I could not collect enough
to feed myself and little Jesse.
Most of Husband's cases
mining accidents. No hospital.
No shelter. In my spare moments I'd nurse
fractured ribs, pierced intestines
beneath needles of sleet. Some
I didn't think could live an hour—
ragged hands clenched, knees drawn up
to faces set with pain. I sang or hummed,
nobody died as long as there was music.
I felt like a bird warbling beside
the battleground outside Vicksburg
and longed to hear from Brother
who'd taught me Mendelssohn.

Come spring we moved to Boise Basin—
deep snow and axe-proof ice.
Husband a considerate gentleman
when he left the bottle alone.
I met a friend I'd taught school with
and waited her tables, washing dishes
in her boarding place, in exchange
baby and I received bed and kitchen scraps.
Martin Gay, a miner there, tipped
a gold nugget. Paid me another to sing
A Midsummer Night's Dream...
Drunk most of the time, Dr. Dillon
taunted baby till she cried, abusing her
if she didn't cease. I fled—gale winds,
snow thick as barley mash, and husband followed.

He swore off liquor, I took him back.
Smallpox broke out.
He saved many, but feared he'd offend
the saloonmen who ran the town if he didn't imbibe
now and then, and soon drank most of the time.
I worked tables where Martin Gay boarded.
When mining fever subsided, I nursed
our minister's invalid wife.
She wanted all of Mendelssohn every night,
I hummed without accompaniment
—oh to hear from Brother,
hadn't General Lee surrendered? Husband
binged for weeks on end, no song
I knew could heal him.
A judge who later became governor
secured me a divorce. The minister
in whose house I nursed was called
to Portland's largest church, his bedridden wife
wouldn't go without me.

Mr. Gay and I corresponded.
He sent me hymns, the measures soft,
accents falling where expected, giving
a sense of fulfillment, completion, rest—
I grew fond of his flowery signature.
But each time I called for my mail

I prayed: let this one be from Brother.
In my employer's brick sanctuary,
Martin Gay and I married—
seven-year-old Jesse at my side.
I sang at my own wedding. Later,
visiting Mr. Gay's home place near Eugene,
I heard his sister tell a neighbor:
Martin has married a sweet-voiced widow.

We've moved twenty-one times in fourteen years,
which might be why
Brother's letters have never reached me.

Wedding photo of George Armstrong Custer and Elizabeth (Libbie) Clift Bacon Custer, married February 9, 1864.

At First, Judge Bacon was Reluctant to allow his Daughter to be Courted by the Son of a Blacksmith

"My dear 'Beloved Star'—
   "Old fellow with the golden curls, save them from the barber's.
When I'm old I'll have a wig made from them."
                        —*Libbie to Armstrong, December 23, 1863*

   "The bridal gifts were exhibited in a room adjoining the drawing
room.... They included: Silver dinner service from the 1ˢᵗ Vermont Cavalry, Silver Tea Sett, 7 pieces, 7ᵗʰ Michigan Cavalry. Silver card case, card
receiver, silver cup, sugar spoons, berry spoons, thimble (gold-lined),
napkin-ring.
   "Two white silk fans, sandal wood. Mrs. Browning's poems; 'Whispers to the Bride'; 'Female Poets.' Knit breakfast shawl; Mosaic chest-
stand of Grand Rapids Marble."
                        —*Rebecca Richmond to Mary Richmond, February 1864,*
                        Grand Rapids, Michigan.

Jésus et Marie, ma force et ma gloire

Jesus and Mary, my strength and my glory

—Motto of the Sisters of the Holy Names of Jesus and Mary

The Matter of the Raspberries

Mother Veronica of the Crucifix Petitions*
the Bishop of Montreal, St. Mary's Academy,
Portland, Oregon, 1865

i.

Oh, the oppressive green of trees
so dark as to appear black,
the wrong river, wrong mountains
tethered to a ceiling of unremitting rain.
When I sailed down the St. Lawrence
shadowed by the Laurentians, crossed
Panama, boarded a coastal steamer northward
landing in the Lord's farthest untilled field,
I felt shut inside a cellar.
But Sadness, it is said, the eighth capital sin;
and as I looked for diamond crosses
in the Willamette, the rosy cheeks
of the Holy Infant in a Cascade sunrise,
the wailing of urgent need filled my ears.

I learned long before I was missioned west
that our Customs Book does not cover
every detail of every incident;
what is right is what puts the heart to rest. Yet
what solution to apply to all these
none-too-clean children of the forest
and other nameless waifs
thrown at night across the convent fence?

ii.

Long ago, as a newly promised novice,
I was sent with another sister
to study teaching methods: We sang
hymns appropriate to the day, memorized
lives of the Saints, facts from the Bible,
scribing in perfect penmanship,
edifying examples drawn from Scripture.
We resided at *Maison de la Providence*

and, to avoid distraction, traveled
in a closed carriage. En route, we intoned
the Little Office of the Virgin.
For fortification we cleaved
to our Novice Master's rules:
to speak in low voices,
to receive no visitors,
to always be together,
to love to admonish
one another, never
to speak on the street. And *never*
to forget: although our fathers
were of pure French origin,
we were subjects to the enemy
in our own country.

Some problematic moments occurred:
On the avenue, the Cathedral Canon stopped
to chat, we lowered our eyes,
was it wrong to ignore a man
who would be Bishop? We had obeyed
The Rule so our hearts were peaceful.
Then there was the matter of the raspberries:
As we walked with Mother General
in the convent garden, she offered handfuls.
Our rules forbade eating outside
the refectory. Unobtrusively we carried
these morsels to our cell where they beckoned.
Though hungry, we denied ourselves
each red sweet; opened the window, casting
the raspberries over the sill.
Dilemma, solution.
None of us doubted our road to perfection.

iii.

And now—days spent teaching, nights
scrubbing floors, re-patching Holy Habits—
it is not unusual during morning inspections
or going to open the academy gate, to find
a different fruit: those tiny, wailing bundles.
Brought inside, given ministrations
of warm water and soap, then baptized.

Named for a saint, surnamed
for their origin: Mary Brigit East
appeared on the Vigil of the Epiphany.
Clement LePort, found under the porch.
Last night's visitation, Margaret Redeemed,
thrown with such force her face
bruised and bloodied. Flickering
only for a few hours, some of them,
Our Savior culls these flowers
who have opened beneath his smile.
Today our little-girl-of-the-Epiphany
transplanted to the heavenly garden.

Monsignor: salvaging and preparing
for the grave so many cast-off fruit—
did I not offer myself freely for these tasks?
I lay their ransomed souls before you
and recommend them to your prayers. But how,
each time, to put my troubled heart to rest?

Hedwidge Onesime Davignon (b. 1820), St. Mathias, Quebec

Je Mets Ma Confiance

Ja mets ma confiance,
Vierge, envotre secours.
Servez-moi de defense,
Prenez soin de mes jours.

—St. Louis-Marie Grignion de Montefort of Brittany,
founder of the Daughters of Wisdom, c. 1800

Mother Veronica of the Crucifix, circa 1850.

Sisters of the Holy Names of Jesus and Mary Oregon Province foundresses, circa 1859.
Back row, l-r: Sister Mary Febronia, Sister Mary of the Visitation, Sister Mary Perpetua,
Sister Mary of Calvary, Sister Mary Agathe, Sister Mary Margaret, Sister Mary of
Mercy, Sister Mary Florence, Sister Mary Julia.
Front row, l-r: Sister Francis Xavier, Sister Mary Arsenius, Sister Mary Alphonse.

How We Got On
Reverend T. L. Jones (b. 1841), Portland, Oregon

Prospecting: hard to explain
how I could barely make wages
for weeks, then strike a pocket,
rocking out in one shovelful
of rich dirt found between granite seams.
For years I sang, *Gold*
does not tarnish, silk does not rot.
It is said: Things come to the young—
and all manner of wealth came to me
against all odds. As winter came on,
trekking to Idaho's Orofino
I traded saddle horse,
pack horse, what money I had
for only partial interest in a likely looking gulch.
Broke and without grub
I dug through snow, through
six feet of clay to gravel
that I thawed by wood fire—
it just happened
to be a rich piece of ground. I kept on:
staked a claim, rocked out
at hundreds of dollars a day, sold it,
found another. I swear
I could taste the sweetness
of pay dirt in sluice water.
Through more than one severe storm
I wandered snow blind, feet frozen, sacks
of gold dust weighing me down like iniquities
until I could not go on. But as if
there were lamps on my feet and
a light unto my path, I invariably stumbled
into a wigwam where merciful red men
provided venison, moccasins, and
exact directions out of the canyon
onto a trail to Lewiston, Grand Ronde,
Fort Klamath, where I finally found
priceless treasure.

She had fire opal hair
and smooth-as-moonstone skin. One of sixteen
whose father died when a grizzly clawed
off an arm. Mary Baird and I married
New Year's '68. I kept on prospecting
but the more we thought,
the more the mere making of money
seemed a waste of life.
We joined the Methodists,
memorized their hymnals, walked six miles
to sermons. I'd never prayed in public before;
had a terror of speaking up, but swore
I'd give testimony if called upon.
When chosen to preach,
a year's salary: one hundred eighty dollars
(some of that taken in horse feed)
—what I'd made in a single day of mining.

How'd we get on?
Occasional windfalls: An elder left us
his boots, which I patched for my wife.
We never spent a cent on meat—I was
a crack shot, deer hams always hung
in our smokehouse. Bear
gave us lard and surprisingly delicious bacon.
We let no seed fall by the way.
I've been married sixty years,
which seems but days.
The hardest twelve minutes of my life?
My first sermon, beginning
"He who loves money will never have enough."
Then, befuddled by dread,
I repeated over and over:
"Never confuse the flicker of gold for the lantern
of righteousness—what communion
has darkness with light?" And ended,
"From this world we carry nothing out."
For that I was given a circuit seventy by
ninety-five miles, sixteen preaching stations,
all records and church property.
By the grace of God I built a fine sanctuary.

Like all earthly treasure, its hinges
broken into by rust, its windows by thieves,
the altar cloth my wife wove corrupted by moths.
In time even salt lost its savor, but
for the sweet treasures of heaven
I have never lost my taste.

Reverend T. L. Jones and Mary Baird Jones later in life.

T. L. Jones (center) as a young man mining in Idaho.

The Grass Hunter

Justin Gibson, 1867

May 12: Left Missouri full of enthusiasm and same lure of adventure
that prompted enlistment in Union Army. Everything disposed of—
except livestock, wagon, and prized lead mares. Reached Plattsmouth
after 2 days' walk. Rain, grass sparse along the road. Chummed up with
Wagonmaster's brother Kirk, his wife, and wife's younger sister, Lillian.
Salt Creek. Plum Creek. Level country, made good time. Ft. Kearny:
Scattered timber. Kirk injured by mule kick, helped his women with team.
Carried 4 buckets of water for Lillian who has hair the color of spring
butter. When her eyes traced bayonet scar across my cheek, I imagined the
wound kissed.

Julesburg: Rockies (weeks away) coming into view—jagged, majestic,
purple. Grass cropped nearly to the root. Rumors of a Nez Perce outbreak
and swarming Sioux.

May 21: Kirk some better. Asked if I would pick him green jimsonweed
for tea.

June 10: Came to grass and good water, then crossed South Platte—a
sluggish stream. Best grazing occupied by ranchers, their stock having
mowed every meadow. Kirk's wife taken ill. Reached the North Fork:
Willow and cottonwood our only feed.

Today stopped over to tar wagon wheels, repair harness. Kirk able to
hobble around. Sick myself this a.m. Cold wind. Traveled through knee-
high grass most of the afternoon. Crossing hills of scattered pine, helped
Lillian collect wood—run off her feet caring for Kirk and sister. Acciden-
tally touched her shoulder and had to grab for breath.

Medicine Bow Mountains offered only the dramatic green of lichened
rocks. Not much grazing in sight. Picked pennyroyal, gave to Lillian.
Snowbanks. Noon: reached tolerable grass.

June 18: Kirk's wife improving. Helped Kirk locate stand of jimson-
weed. Tea helps lift the Mrs.'s asthma.

July 4: Arrived Ft. Halleck. Lilly asked if I would accompany her to
factor's house for mail. Crossed pole bridges, paid toll. No post for any one
of our party. No grass. Ferried over North Platt. Ground so stony and dry
hard to believe it was ever green. Four miles off road on rocky trail came to

some roughage, no water fit to drink. Preponderance of sage. Traded spare rifle for 1 sack oats. Encountered first Indians: 3 gaudily dressed bucks ahorseback who carried on guttural conversation with much pointing.

Today our train broke into 2 groups on account of scarcity of grass. Joined Kirk, wife, and Lil. Spent the a.m. trying to catch her gaze. No wood. No grazing near but got some by traveling with Kirk's and my stock 1 mile off trail. Hauled water.

Lil admired the peacock burl anchored in my hatband. Kirk sent grass hunters ahead, myself included. Thunder heard all day. Found grass for horses but hard to get at. Melted snow for water. p.m.: Lilly browned beans for coffee, offering me a pot with biscuits and precious dab of molasses. Hills striped with green of dwarf cedars.

Last night fed stock grain kept for emergencies. Today: Found grass for horses, but too short for cattle. Kirk's wife still on sick list: Fever, drowsiness, relentless thirst. Lilly alarmed.

August 1: Crossed into Idaho. Flax in first valley bottom, but scattered. Reached banks of Snake. Kirk lost a mule while crossing, Lil quite shaken. Kirk said he had looked away only for a moment to help Lilly who'd torn off her boot heel. Kirk's wife some improved. Nooned on good grass.

Followed riverbed to American Falls which could be heard 2 days away. Kirk's wife very low—vision blurred, difficulty passing water. Traveled until dark. Grass here nearly eaten out. Traded tinned peaches for quantity of oats. Followed tributary to plenty of rye and willow. Lil's eyes, red from alkali dust, flashed like sapphires. Kirk and I chased stock away from stand of Jimson weed gone to berry, sure to cause cattle to loco and stampede over cliffs.

Detail of army scouts stopped our train. Terse words exchanged: War fever among the Klamath. Stomp of restless hoofs and crunch of grazing stock kept me from sleep.

August 14: Withering heat and clogging sand. Road steep. Indifferent grass, water holes few. Kirk's wife delirious from fever. Lil still down about mule. Gave her the peacock burl from my hat to cheer her. Chanced into elk. Shot 2; one bull, one cow. 3 days to good grazing. Distant dust devils assumed guise of smoke signals.

August 20: Slow progress. Hill out of riverbed worst so far, heavy pulling, pure rock in steps 2 feet high. Evening: while on guard duty, talked with Lilly. Stood so close wisps of her hair blew into my mouth. When Kirk came to fetch her, he gave me the news: Bannocks holed up in our vicinity.

Hoped to reach Boise by nightfall, wind blowing too hard for travel. Too dark to hunt for grass. Lead mares poor in flesh and spirit. Wagons corralled, chained together. Trunks, bedding piled up to form barricade behind wheels. Extra guards posted. Kirk's wife: fever finally broke. Kirk, a genius with Jew's harp, played as we sang camp songs to drown out wind and wolf call. Rousted early and on our way.

Hired pasture for 25 cents per head. Lilly excused herself from dinner to write home. Got up nerve to ask if her missive was to a sweetheart. Said letter was to sister's in-laws—parents and brother. Forded Payette River, grass salty. Camped as storm set in, hail the size of buckshot. Kirk's wife: weak, but no worse.

A sort of miracle: traded elk hide for oats. Drove all day, came to lush slough grass which stock would not eat. Re-crossed Snake. Next morning, 2 mules missing at first light. Assumed redskins had injunned up on them, but found at water hole nearby. Word went out: we are now in Oregon.

Burnt River destitute of grass. Shelled out last oats to lead mares. Got bunch grass by going up mountain. Lilly helped, scything and carrying armfuls, said haying a relief—her sister can get no ease, complains terribly. "Who are you?" she asked of Lilly this a.m.

Sept. 1: Powder River. Morning bitter as November, but state of nerves improving as rumor has it Indians gone to ground for winter. Camped within hearing of quartz mill. Blue Mountains, some snow on pine tops, mostly drizzle. Grueling climb routed along precipices, up and down steep pitches, but good grass at day's end. Went with Lills to Canyon City for post. None. Spoke seriously to her. Made decision to speak with Kirk for her hand after we strike Oregon City.

Sept 20: Crossed John Day River, uphill all the way. Cattle and horses weak. Ranchers furnished grazing, 10 cents a head. Lilly, still some despondent over mule, contemplates returning to Missouri as soon as sister's health returns. Will take Barlow Road across shoulder of Mt. Hood. Lead mares show effects of heavy tugging.

Cheered Lilly with regimental songs. Crossed Deschutes by way of toll bridge. Down western Cascades to Oregon City. Cold showers, but abundant grass ½ mile off trail. A relief after months of unfenced expanses of sage. Many improved farms so grass scant as we approached. A blessing: 1 pack animal our 5 month journey's only casualty.

September 22: Kirk informed me he would lay-over in town until wife improves and he can replace mule. Lillian, he said, must stay on as nurse.

Lilly looked despondent, adamantly promising to write. Shook hands goodbye in view of everyone, could not decipher her expression. When her small fingers skidded across the hairs of my arm, wished I'd the gall to grab and kiss her.

Crossed a wide murky Willamette with cheerless heart, took west course following Indian trail over succession of steep ridges. Dense forests and brushwood enveloped with smoke, large fires to the south despite constant drizzle. Unable to see surrounding country. Horses unfit for such rough service, one gave out completely.

Like yesterday, steep ascents, road obstructed by felled trees. Passed through tract of charred logs. At Elk City checked post.

A toilsome journey struggling through cherry thicket. Siletz River 40 feet wide, 3 feet deep, boulders breaking rapid current. Crossing, ascended bank into handsome prairie. Soil rich, grass luxurious where not completely choked by fern 8 feet high. Made final camp.

One neighbor to the west—Scotsman with dairy herd, wife, five homely daughters, one son very sickly. Promised to check post for me when he went to Elk City.

October 16: Today commenced building shelter. Imagined Lilly's tiny hands stitching curtains for the one window. Could smell her biscuits and butter-colored hair.

Nov. 3: Band of Regulars headed for King's Valley camped here for 1 night. Gave 25 cents per horse to graze. Asked Lieutenant-in-command for news from Oregon City of members of overland train. He said that Wagonmaster and brother Kirk had headed for better grass in Rogue River country. And Kirk's wife's sister? I asked; had she gone back to Missouri? The Lieutenant said that he wasn't aware that Kirk's new bride had a sister. When I regained my voice, I summoned the courage to ask the new wife's name. The Lieutenant could not recall ever having heard it.

Oregon City, 1867.

On the Second Through Train

The Widow Jones (Sarah Ann Givens)
Recalls Her Honeymoon, May 10, 1869

According to family lore
Father came to Indiana
to attend a friend's wedding,
and seeing a girl descend
the stairs twined in a crocheted shawl
blue as the wisteria
veiling grandmother's veranda,
he said, *that's the one*—my mother,
which is how they met and married.

Sundays,
offended by our German
Lutheran pastor's habit of rebuking
by name
wrongdoers from the pulpit,
father broke away from church
and home, heading west
into the cholera summer of '52.

When I started New Harmony School,
I studied his letters
postmarked Sacramento.
If he joined the Union,
fought the North, or not at all,
no one knew. Talk had it
he built bed-roads, then
Pullman Palace cars.
(A railroad man, made of money, maybe
he'd send for me!)
Mother always said
my heart-shaped face favored his,
that fact plus name, place, and love
for Grandma's pendulous
heaven's own porch vine
all I knew of him.

May 10th of my seventeenth year
(descending the same stairs
wearing a newly crocheted shawl),
I married a Union vet in an ink
blue uniform—Robert, my sturdy Scot.
Though not Lutheran, my family
took him in. How could they not—
a battle signature red as the mustache
he grew to hide it
scrawled across his upper lip.

O my wedding day: the golden spike
driven into the iron trail's
last laid rail: like man and wife
(Jones, R. D., and Sarah A.),
Eastern coastline and California
forever linked. My surprise
honeymoon trip: passage
on the second through train,
Terra Haute to Sacramento, where
a liveryman knew my father.
He seemed to have remarried—
that newsy letter nowhere among my primers.

When our buggy pulled up
to his lean-to with one goat tethered
in a field of five establishments
called Roseville, Father
had just commenced his supper.
Tin spoon dropping in tin bowl,
he grabbed my waist, lifting me
off the ground: Daughter,
he demanded, Who is this man?
He knew nothing of my wedding
or my longed-for trip west.
Florid-faced, step uncertain,
hands wobbly as legs of an hour-old calf;

with my new husband as my witness,
never had I felt such a jolt
of pity, like a woman trying to care
for every abandoned animal along the road.

The Gift of Granny Wintersteen
New Harmony, Kansas, 1869

No matter what finery she's married in,
my instructions—how to put it to good use—
the same. That gown, a wealth of fabric, lace,
buttons, baleen—even the hem thread can
be reused, hand-stitching the first layette:
little vests made of a bride's soft underskirt,
trimmed with bodice lace on sleeves and neck.
Baby's waistband from mother's own—always
feather-stitch the edges—tightly secured
around our wee one's stomach (so when
she grows up, her waist will lace
to an hourglass shape on her wedding day).

Disparage not the nuptial dress of flour sacking;
cut and neatly hemmed, the best diapers.
Next, baby's yard-long skirts making eight thicknesses
of cloth elaborately tucked, ruffled,
trimmed with twelve safety pins pulled tight.
Infant's outer wear: a calico slip
—starched it stays clean longer. From the bridal
skirt, a bib cut, then quilted to better
collect moisture; a tiny tight-fitting cap
completes baby's home dress. To each bride

I give these instructions, a portfolio
of patterns, one lead blue sketching pencil.
In small script on the backside as if in afterthought:
Dear One, None of us knows how long the watch
is wound. Always save a yard—maybe two—
of fabric, bringing comfort to a neighbor when
you line her infant's coffin.

Lucy Ann Shows Off Her Scrapbook and Talks About the Art of Regulating Temperatures

Lucy Ann Henderson Deady (b. Feb. 26, 1835)

i.

My first year in Oregon I did nothing
but shiver. Wet wood fires
make choking smoke and worse bread;
we were ragged—boiled wheat with peas our staples.
Mother cried, but I wasn't sorry
to see Father hurry south to Sutter's Fort.
If luck found him, he said,
he'd send me to school.
I was twelve and sociable and longed
for lessons, not scowling Indians
whose nudity near paralyzed me or
skies dark as Egypt and sea-drenching rain;
our skin turned bone white
under every lightning whip.

Oregon City Academy: filled
with fine furniture, ornate oil lamps; the banister
so sable and smooth I petted it.
My school chums wore velvet mantelets,
silk chemises, sleeves enriched by ribbons with
Maltese lace at their wrists. I had none
of this. All the same, I greened
every eye with the courtship
of Judge Matthew Deady.

Back then, men wondered why
a girl wasn't married if she was sixteen
and single. The Judge—a towering
Irishman—delivered me a note
from a boy I'd met at a piano social.
More interested in the letter's bearer
than the letter, I didn't keep it.
When they saw the Judge with me at church,

my chums helped sew my wedding costume
from their own flounces: a skirt
pointed in front, fastened in back,
a Dutch neck like a Rembrandt;
kid slippers and kid gloves, a hat
with silk streamers for a veil—here, a swatch
of white ribbon, the first thing I saved.

ii.

Housekeeping setup in a one-room with
lean-to kitchen—all mine! I was seventeen.
I could fry meat, but had never
roasted it. When Judge presented me
with an oven, I couldn't confess
I'd never lived in a home with a stove.
Proud of his girl-wife, Judge invited guests.
I lit the fire box, put in a venison rump.
When I cranked open the heavy door, smoke
choked the cottage. Taking charge,
the Judge cooked our first meal,
our second, and so on—until
I learned the art
of regulating temperatures.

iii.

When Judge rode the southern circuit alone,
I worried. Crossing Rogue River at high water,
he met countless ruffians: one claimed
unceasing voices called him
to California; holding out his pistol, he begged
a five dollar loan.
The Judge gave it. Years later,
a lawyer in high hat and swallow tails
blocked our door, demanding:
remember me?
then returned money he claimed he owed.

Here, I have it in my scrapbook:
A five dollar bill bookmarked in a sheaf
of verse printed in England: *to Judge Deady,*
who helped me get my start,
and his flamboyant autograph, see

—*J* and *Q* like thrown lariats, *L*'s
like gallows—*Joaquin Miller*, defender
of despots, poet of the Sierras. Pages
of souvenirs: news clippings, a copy
of the Judge's speech
at the iron wedding when rail lines
first bridged the Snake, a poem
where every word begins with
the letter *p*, portraits of myself,
our three sons, Mother. Scraps
of a life clipped, pasted, forever
saved—

as he saved me.

Lucy Henderson Deady.

Judge Matthew P. Deady.

Kelp

Lucy Stevens, Ocean House, Newport, Oregon, 1875

Who can account for what catches
in memory's cogs?
I must have been ten. Little Theo Olsen
and I were on the beach waiting
for gristle-faced Bill White
to sail the mail boat down the Yaquina—
he lived on the wharf, unpainted shanty
below the cleat-studded plank road
that struggled up the yellow sand bluff:
one door, one window, a waist-high slide
on the backside to throw out
peelings and dishwater.
I often wondered how smoke
could ribbon up his stovepipe or how
the slide opened and shut
when he was in Elk City fetching the post—
mother said she surely didn't know.

We children ran past his shack
toward Whale Rock, jumping whitened
water-worn driftwood, log-to-log.
There she sat on a stump knitting socks:
A little brown walnut husk with one eye,
if she had another name I never knew it; *Dummy*
came south with the Indian folk
when allowed to leave their reservation.
They camped and fished and clammed below
our town named for a place
in Rhode Island—the boardinghouse Father ran
named for its famous hotel.
Dummy and the bronze people
lived like kelp flooding in with the tide.
She couldn't speak any tongue
not even Native; could she understand English?
She gestured, made queer croaky squawks.
Wanting to know how she'd lost her eye,

we pointed, made pained faces,
held our hands out at various heights: how old?
With a language all her own—
vocabulary of pantomime, sharp looks
with her one coal eye, motions of
hands and head—her stories better than
our Christmas tableau, which Mother wrote.

Dummy told us: The height she was now,
sixteen times she shivered, that many winter fires,
so age sixteen when hundreds of boats and horses
left the river's mouth, no room for her
in a canoe; she'd had to swim.

It took time to get her ideas straight;
if she sensed bewilderment, she'd retrace
her tale with some new gesture.
Try and try we could never fool her
into thinking we understood.
Try and try, little Theo Olsen
could not unnerve Dummy with the pop
or bang of a dried seaweed bladder—
she was deaf as a stump.

Feet frozen, belly cramped,
she had pulled herself ashore,
too exhausted to stand, she fell
onto thorns, puncturing her eye.
Oh, what pain! We cringed
at the fright of it as we sat
on the log next to her, running
beach sand through our toes.
Three cold terrible months until her eye healed.
Dummy couldn't make anything like a word,
but her squawks conveyed everything.
We never tired of her tales.

She went back to knitting socks
—odd, since she wore no shoes.
We walked back to the wharf
past Mailman White's bleak shack

with its blue ribbon of smoke.
Theo Olsen pointed to the waist-high slide
on the shack's backside: Where Dummy "trawls"
in and out, Theo said—he meant "crawls."

Later, Mother wrung her hands when I told her
about his terrible elocution.

Newport, Oregon, in the early days.

Gifted to Miss Lydia Corum upon her Marriage to Anderson Deckard

Amanda Gardener Johnson (b. 1833, Slave State of Missouri), Albany, Oregon

i.

In Clay County—Little Dixie—
not far from Liberty City,
on hard ochre clay
tobacco leaves sprawled
large as mule skins.
At sundown, Miss Lydia collared
and kept me indoors
rocking her baby no matter
how oppressive the heat.
As the sun's forge dropped
into the Missouri, igniting heaven,
Miss Lydia twisted a soft finger
into my dimple—mirror of her own—
like a key into a lock, singing, *'Manda,
don't let God catch you
sharpening the tips of your smile.*

I'd six sisters, five brothers, all
born at Olde Oaks, none
sold or bartered for, all given
by Master to his young folks.
Barely a tot, when he presented me
to his eldest, Mrs. Corum.
At age seven, I was given
to her daughter; when she first saw me,
Miss Lydia's eyes hummed,
pinning my heart forever to her breast.

ii.

Fear of being sold the one shadow
on my happiness—Mr. Deckard could drink
or be unlucky at cards prompting
a liquidation of slaves. Those auctions!
Like the sale of Kentucky horses, except

after running a finger down a field hand's leg
bidders could ask him questions.
The high prices that somber-skinned
house girls commanded
turned to ice the sweat
pooling at the base of my throat.

I was nineteen when Master
decided to emigrate. When
the cotton gin owner offered
twelve hundred dollars for me,
Master slammed the double oak doors
on him and gave me a choice: freedom
to stay with my people, which I yearned for,
or to go with his family to Oregon
where slaves could not be held.
The echo of the auctioneer's bawl
rattled my thoughts: Without Miss Lydia,
any bad white man could claim I'd been stolen,
bring me up on charge after charge
while doing unto me as he would his livestock.

iii.

I chose a six months' walk,
Clay County to Willamette Valley:
dust and graves and heat and high water,
shaggy shouldered buffalo, dowel-
legged antelope, more graves and sage
and Indians and smoke
from buffalo chip campfires
where I cooked for Miss Lydia's children.
Any number of freed slaves crossed
that year growing unmindful
of curfew. I held my breath
as day turned to night, but
neither sheriff nor cholera found me.

I got work at Magnolia Flour Mill,
a short morning trek through tar-
colored, shoe-pulling mud
on the Confederate side of town.
Always home by sunset, though

most days in Oregon, clouds curtained
the sun's path, the danger hour
difficult to determine.
Would I be thrown in jail if found
on the streets after dusk?

Imagine my surprise at earning
the same wage as a white overseer
back home. On my day off,
if no Deckard needed nursing,
I strode along the hedge of incense cedar
segregating the white two-story homes
of Union sympathizers until magnetic force
pulled me back to Deckards' before dark.
Why did I think Union newspapers
might have word of my kin?
So many prayers and letters unanswered.

iv.

When Miss Lydia died,
I married a blacksmith
— a freed slave who came west
the same year that I did—
I wore a brown silk dress and long
brown silk gloves;
the Magnolia Mill owner ground
a special run of flour for my cake.
—A strange crop, wheat: fields the color
of a white man's hair, the harvest silent
of work hollers; only the whisper
of hand sickles, like the dying's last breath.

After thirty years, I lost Benjamin
and went back
to the only family I had. If you call
on me, Miss Lydia's granddaughter
will answer your knock. When I go
to town—where many still hold
the word of a freed slave as valueless—
I'm always home before the sun
falls behind the sword-topped hills.
Sometimes in the wind, the voice

of Miss Lydia beseeches: *Lord,*
What sharpened this sweet child's
smile into a scythe?

No matter how harsh the lye soap,
I cannot scrub away the notion
that Miss Lydia owned me, or explain
the way her mink-colored eyes,
even in death, forever claw at my heart.

The only known photograph of Amanda Gardener Johnson.

As Granny Wintersteen Unpacks Her Midwife's Case, She Realizes that She Has Forgotten Her Collapsible Shovel Used for Sterilizing Linens by Fire

Boise, 1877

smelling salts
witch hazel
foxglove
verbena
whiskey

measuring glass
pocket scales

Booklet: "Anatomical Tables &
    Illustrations of the Theory &
    Practice of Midwifery"

membrane perforator
    with ebony handle
Blundell's forceps
horsehair fillet
vectis
cranioclast
hook and crochet
scissors
calipers

bedpan
dilator
nipple shield
feeding cup
feeding bottle
syringe
enema
wooden stethoscope
lantern
bleached calico
carbolic acid
sweet oil
corn starch
silver nitrate 2% solution
glass rod
bear grease

unfinished linen sampler 8" x 8",
    6 skeins of colored silk
    thread: "*Well begun is half
    done,*" with a rice running
    stitched border.

Kloh-Kloh

Lotta Gilham's Mother Talks about the Early Years,
Tillamook Country, Oregon, 1870s

As a bride, I helped your father
manage the oyster beds.
Our nearest neighbors a Native village—
driftwood shacks spanned
the beach of a fishhook-shaped spit.
Almost no visitors,
clippers entering Eel Grass Bay
prevented from landing by storms
so severe all assembled on deck
to make their last confessions. On clear days
the sight of men clad in animal skins
turned sails away from a village
of ravenous dogs and children
in cedar houses and cedar skirts
on cedar mats plagued by fleas.

The first discord came over oysters.
We paid the women twelve and a half cents
a bushel, stuffed in gunny bags and tied
for transport should a ship successfully land.
But Natives could not understand
why they shouldn't pluck *kloh-kloh*
from the salt marsh and eat their fill.
Because they don't belong to you,
we told them. Use your wages
to buy food, we instructed. Few
took our advice to heart.

The second discord over pastry flour
at the general store owned by a Portuguese
the Natives called Chipped Nose—
his merchandise culled from shipwrecks:
bars and bars of beeswax traded
for canvas and coffee and gaily printed calico.
He married South Wind, an Indian girl
who wore a spruce root bonnet and carried

a soft rush basket of keepsakes:
Chinese coins, deer teeth, the left front hoof of an elk.
She rubbed seal fat into her braids and when
the sun shone Chipped Nose counted rainbows
in the black ropes that swung below her waist.
He was wealthy compared to the rest of us
and lavished his wife with gifts. Anything
South Wind admired, he gave her.
One day when she ran her hands
through the barrel of pastry flour,
he put it away for her—wouldn't sell a cupful.
All we had for cakes and pies
was coarse and brown and riddled with grit
from a worn-down grindstone.
We thought it odd when South Wind's
ragged sisters enjoyed good health
and she fell into decline.
Their shaman prescribed elk marrow, but
Chipped Nose wouldn't allow such things.
Only white flour and white sugar, even
white chocolate which South Wind
had no taste for, though she put white parings
in a clam shell kept in her cattail basket.

When she died, Chipped Nose wept unceasingly.
South Wind's funeral attended by Natives
and whites from miles around. Lookout Rock
is where the Indian dead were placed
under upturned canoes, but Chipped Nose
demanded a Catholic service, interring his wife
near his store. In the custom of her people
he buried her belongings beside her:
bolt after bolt of gingham she'd admired; combs
carved from walrus tusks, everything
she'd ever owned or wished for;
the grave enlarged,
the barrel of pastry flour thrown in;
her mother's wooden boiling trough,
clam shell spoons, a stick
to beat mussels from rocks,
all her basketry and, since she'd not
been buried beneath a canoe to travel in,

every empty oyster shell—because the *kloh-kloh*
would turn to snipes and bear her through the dark.
The next day her relatives—
Scrub Whale, Auntie Blue Jay, and Steelhead—
knocked down their houses, built rafts
with the lumber, buried their fires,
and left. After a while
in the place where they had been,
a strange grass—stems firm as elk teeth
—grew to the sky and tides
the color of blood rolled in.

Wishham Bride, Tlakluit Indian Woman.

Cutting Her Out from the Flock

Wagonwheel George, Cold Creek, Montana, 1888

Always handle ladies the same
as livestock. When a team of fillies
bedecked in the latest boulevard fashions
stampedes the plank walkways of Billings,
air your chamber pot out of sight, then
saunter 'round to the hitch-racks lining Main.
Remember how Shep works the ewes then
cuts one from the flock? Don't let
the gals bunch together,
keep 'em moving and don't scare
your lamb by barking.
Don't rush her, let her have
her way unless she breaks
for freedom. Like buying a horse
give your lady the once-over:
Born to a range mare, but carries
her head like a Hamiltonian?
Hide sleek, hair chestnut, body slender,
legs (what you can see of them) long?
If you take her dancing, all the better
to inspect her fetlocks, eyes, nose, and
especially her teeth— a full string
of pearls, none long or yellow or missing.

Crazy as a barb pony?
Harder to rope than a bumblebee?
You're not looking for flashy
or fool's gold, but a soul like Old Baldy,
the lead cow you'd never sell.
Sure, she might pull a pout, but
like your best roping horse, your future wife
needs to be a steady plugger.
Does she wheeze?
Of the temperament to take
a hunk of your hide? Skittish and snorting
with dissatisfaction? As to her eyes,
there comes the question: dark or light?

Remember Shep's marbled blues?
Hair color? Like herd dogs, ebonies
prove the hardest workers.
When estimating female character,
the wilder, the more faithful—
the harder to break, the more desirable;
a gal who'll give you her last ounce
of strength. Forget the locoed,
the jumpy, or unusually dumb, probably headed
for a bender of running into buttes
or over cliffs. A locoed woman's
sweet song soon turns
to something between the harangue
of a blue-tail fly and a diamondback's rattle.
If you don't want dreams filled with serpents,
give the locoed wide wagon room.

The sum essence of it all:
so she's not long on looks or faster
than her sister; she's dependable,
chunky but wise, clumsy but turns
on a silver dollar—coolheaded and sure-footed
is what'll save you. She'll jog trot when
a blizzard strikes, facing into it
all the way home; your feet
so numb you have to dismount, cling
to her mane, clutch at her bridle
following afoot in order to keep warm.
She'll never miss a step, steady up steep hills,
around cutbacks where if she slipped you'd
fall to an icy death. Even if you can't see
to steer, nothing rattles her, not even
the small mite of bad language needed
to encourage her on.

So suppose you cut her from the herd,
get engaged in record time, but
discover there's some meanness
in her hide or a poor water supply on her ranch
or her kin's a red-eyed coterie of rascals.
Using the excuse of your daily obscenity,
head out back to the necessary house,

lock yourself in with a bottle
of refreshment strong enough to cure
the snakebite of melancholia,
take a swig, and heave
a long slow sigh more of relief
than sorrow.

A Good Many Brides Today
are a Pampered Self-Indulgent Lot

Fidelia Munson, near Boise, 1893

Printed wedding invitations—we'd never heard of such things; neighbors weren't *invited*, they were *expected*. In my day we had no parties, joy riding, or card playing like the girl who lives next door. Newspapers that printed up these frolicking goings-on? A woman's name should only appear publicly in print twice: married and died. My father didn't hold with dancing—fiddle and squeeze box pandered to baser passions—so I couldn't go. We'd no carnivals or operas. We had hangings. If you'd ever been to one, you would never forget it—crowds as big as if a circus had come to town, only quieter.

When I was young, women and cows had to work hard; no time to indulge in nerves or tantrums. We had plenty of mending and taking care of babies and nursing. I was seven when Father chopped all his toes off of one foot with an axe and had to help earn money until his leg healed. I secured a job cleaning for a sick neighbor. My brothers died young, so my sisters and I took their place. We gathered the wheat, tied it in bundles, and shocked it. I drove the harrow, Father broadcast the grain. I milked morning and night. Mother didn't want her girls to be farmhands, so she taught us to bake and make soap. I begged to go to school, but there wasn't one. Now all my grandchildren are getting good educations. That's a fine thing, though I often wonder: after everybody gets educated, will there be anyone left to do the real work and make a living for the rest of them? Not many brides nowadays can quilt. They can't even take care of babies. Girls of my day trained to be homemakers, not like Marissa next door driving a team of matched bays to the next town to play bridge.

I married at fifteen. Courting done in church or by letter. My wedding dinner consisted of boiled wheat and plenty of milk—with coffee made from burnt rye. I raised nine babies without help. The women of today have but few offspring, which spoils a child. In my youth we took what God sent us without complaint. My husband never made much, all the same we saved. We didn't buy Victrolas. We didn't trade our prairie schooner for a new buggy. Our oxen weren't as fast as horses, but if you gave them time enough they usually arrived where they started for. If you look back over an old-timer's account book, you won't find payments for rent, gas lights, coal, milk, butcher bills, kerosene, or other expenses the bride of today has to meet. I've cooked many a meal and darned many a sock by grease light. We used to save bear fat and, with a twisted bit of rag and a teacup, we made a light that might not have been stylish, but it served the purpose.

As a bride, I worked from daybreak until midnight. Made my own candles. I didn't own a stove until my children were grown. We fried meat over the fire in a long-handled skillet, baked bread in a Dutch oven. I could shoot the heads off of grouse and fish or paddle a canoe as well as an Indian. We made our clothes from wool we'd spun. Back then we couldn't run into a handy store for supplies.

Sometimes I wonder if today's bride is as self-reliant, self-sacrificing, and useful as brides when I was young. There was so much housework that girls didn't get a chance to run around like nowadays. I have neuritis in my thimble finger and that's a pity, because I long to quilt. Marissa next door flatly refuses to own a thimble. If these brides had a life like mine, they would never lack for something to think of when they sit alone beside their fire of an evening. Looking around outside my house in what used to be Juniper Flats before boosters renamed it for an English manor, it hardly seems possible that this town was once a couple of saloons, a blacksmith shop, and some soldiers. Now all the homes have numbers so they'll know where to deliver your daily paper. The very idea of having the particulars of my marriage ceremony written up in the news where everyone could see it, like they did with Marissa's wedding, makes me break out in a sweat. I could say a good deal more about these modern brides if I took a notion, but I was taught that a still tongue makes a wise head, so I'll leave off right here.

Ida Mae Recalls the Broken Plates
of her China Anniversary

Mrs. William Dutton (b. 1860), Heppner, Oregon

I'd have to say
that my Twentieth Anniversary
marked a certain sad symmetry to life.
Our wedding, a big home place affair;
my most valued present, a full set
of gold-banded Haviland.
For so many reasons,
I will never forget the evening before:
Mother directing bridesmaids
as they carried china
up the front steps in laundry baskets,
dish clatter muffled by straw,
covered by bedsheets.
Every plate, cup, saucer edged
in sweetly fluted gold twists
brighter than the wheat-
colored dawn of my wedding day.
My china so pristine I could see
my new husband's sunny cheeks. Faces
of girlhood friends glowed
in the mirror of each plate's rim.

> *I see them still, can only imagine*
> *sultry heat, heavy clouds dark as bruises,*
> *the viciousness of lightning whips,*
> *how a curtain of rain turned*
> *to hail too loud to speak over, hiding…*

Housework hard our first winter,
I cried countless times. As a girl
my only chore to mend and whiten linens.
It took me years to receive praise
for a savory sit-down dinner
for I-don't-know-how-many.

Most folks ran inside, upstairs
watched the bridge go, heard shotgun blasts...

Mother died. We never had children.
As our Twentieth approached, we thought
of adding to our Haviland—gravy boat
or footed cream soup-and-saucer set?
Without Mother, I couldn't decide. In town,
we rented Roberts Hall, draping streamers
in wildflower colors beam to beam,
dining first at the Palace Hotel with
the tinkle of Willow Creek as orchestra.
June, lambing over, all sheep sheared,
bags of wool stored in our loft.
A droughty place, Heppner, but
after a deluge we breathed easier: the breaking
of memory's driest spring. Off we went,
a second wedding trip to Portland;
at the train, a white lake of waving handkerchiefs.

I see them still, can only imagine
sultry heat, heavy clouds dark as bruises,
the viciousness of lightning whips,
how a curtain of rain turned
to hail too loud to speak over, hiding
the roar of water breaking logjams, silt
bleeding over level ground like stain.

Our barn not much damaged, but
you can't imagine the clutter
of wet clothing, sediment, broken chairs.
We returned not to the stench of sheep,
but two hundred rotting corpses.
As men piled bodies up
against our fences, there was no one
I didn't recognize.

Most folks ran inside, upstairs
watched the bridge go, heard shotgun blasts
of houses crashing by, streets seared by cold
mud too deep to walk through, heaps
of debris, trees, timbers, chests of drawers.

Roberts Hall a converted morgue,
our party streamers drooping pitifully
over the porcelain-cold kaolin faces
of girlhood friends. Not enough sheets
for shrouds, not enough dry straw
to cushion the rattle of dirt thrown
atop makeshift coffins. Broken plates,

I see them still, can only imagine

rugs, dinner forks in various patterns;
months before we cleared off the wreckage,
an undertaking unmanageable even for Mother
had she lived to see it.

Gold-rimmed gravy boat, gold-footed soup server;
my china anniversary marked
a dark harmony. Walking down creek,

sultry heat, heavy clouds dark as bruises,

I found two dresses of a toddler drowned
with his parents. I couldn't
help myself: I took them home,
laundered, whitened, ironed each tatted flower,
returning them to one of my bridesmaids,
his grandmother.

Heppner, Oregon, flood, 1903.

How Firm a Foundation

When through the deep waters I call thee to go,
The rivers of woe shall not thee overflow;

That soul, though all hell should endeavor to shake,
I'll never, no never, no never forsake.

You Haven't Asked About My Wedding Or What I Wore

Belle Bishop (b. 186—), Pendleton, Oregon

I remember it like yesterday:
tending my brother's sheep
mornings and nights,
trimming hats for Mother
in between times—so I hardly noticed
when the Judge starting courting.
No one could fathom why
he'd frequent a millinery shop,
as Pendleton had suffered a fresh
rash of robberies and he'd
more pressing concerns—
which was indeed the case.

The Judge owned a prize ox,
Big Ben, who worked laying
rail line, during which time
he was gored by a wild cow.
The Judge loved that ox
more than life, fret for it
kept him from sleep. When
he came in ordering a poke-
style off-the-face bonnet trimmed
in a cherry wreath and two
rows of tucks encircling the brim,
Mother knew he was courting, she just
didn't know who. Some widow,
she said. And when he begged
me to ride out to his
Broken Spoke Ranch and try
my flaxseed poultice on Old Ben's
wounded foreleg, Mother told me
I couldn't refuse. Days later
the Judge bought a leghorn trimmed
in velvet forget-me-nots
sprayed with June roses, asking
if I'd come out and apply

my turpentine bath
to a calf infested with red mite.

All livestock improved, but
I contracted disfiguring poison oak.
A week later, I walked home
from the sunflower-strewn draw
where my brother pastured his ewes, tired
and about out of shoe leather.
My face oozing, my eyes swollen shut;
Mother met me at the door, scolding:
Did I know who'd been waiting
for more than an hour?

Of course there was gossip,
talk's sure as taxes.
I'd be the Judge's third wife,
the first two gave out from exhaustion.

Little Peggy Web, who married
my brother, had lots of stylish clothes;
I had none and asked for her help.
My gown made of pearl pongee,
the skirt a deep kilted flounce.
I wore white kid gloves and white
kid slippers. Mother designed
my headgear, and wouldn't speak
to me for weeks when I refused
to wear a veil. She hadn't
been so vexed since the incident
at Webb's Hardware when
I'd minded the store
while the owner went trading:
patrons on the front porch
sitting atop nail kegs
watched in-coming stages,
betting which coach
ran ahead or behind.
I knew about Mr. Webb's binoculars
and innocently wagered
five dollars taken from the till.

Of course, I won
and when word got around,
the owner and my mother
were sent for. I'd stolen,
I'd gambled—it was years
before I told how I'd won.
I was twenty-two, unmarried,
and now likely to remain so.
Aggrieved, Mother threw up her hands.

My bonnet: a straw lined in silk
with white two-inch-wide streamers.
The ceremony festive, though brief—
as mentioned, our town suffered
a fresh siege of banditry.
With no room at the jail,
the Judge handcuffed
prisoners to lampposts.
Walking from church to street
the aroma of urine
stronger than smelling salts.
My new husband resumed
dispensing justice right after
photographers posed us.

I've never been sorry about the veil,
Looking back, I'd change nothing,
except to do it over
as the groom instead of a bride.
I loved to ride horseback and took
to herding cattle like an Indian.
In those days, long skirts
hobbled women afoot or astride;
and in summer we nearly stewed
under a sweat lodge of hair.
I still have those silly cherry wreath
and velvet forget-me-not bonnets—never
taken from their boxes—trophies,
the last hats I ever trimmed.

Abide with Me

I fear no foe, with Thee at hand to bless:
Ills have no weight, and tears no bitterness:
Where is death's sting? Where, grave, thy victory?
I triumph still, if Thou abide with me.

Brown Cloth-Covered Diary
of Memoranda & Cash Accounts

Emily French, Denver, 1890

Whitewashed Mrs. Frick's cornmeal, 45 cents.
An awful wind of wagging tongues
drove me here. Twenty years married;
he drank, one ugly spell
and failed business followed another.
All my fault until he freed himself for
a new hag and their little one, leaving me
—stiff fingered and graying fast—
to starve or beg. Denver,
10 sheets, washed and mended: $1.50
built a house across Willow Street
from Corbin's Dairy. No well,
the South Platt will have to do.
Laid out a child not five years old,
left without pay. Last night:
another visit from Mr. Lawson. Boiled
ham bones, cabbage, potatoes.
Today, worked for a neighbor lady
exhausted by asthma: big wash,
sewed, ironed, took apart the stove, paid
in kindnesses of *1 sack flour & broken crackers.*
Cleaned her chimney (draws better), had to carry
ten pails, water always riley when it rains;
how well I could live on what they waste,
a day's griddle cakes for Dan and Olive—
Dear Lord, may Ollie have a better life
than mine. Went to the lumberyard for nails
and putty. *Starched 3 skirts, fluted another.*
Came home tired, headache, raw
winds blowing a hurricane. No fire,
poor beds, scarce any covers. Pray
God send me a way to stay at home.
We three sleep together in our own
house again after being so moved around
—our own if I can pay. *Washing: three men's*
work clothes, so dirty: 75 cents, so little.

Here again tonight, John Lawson:
fried potatoes, organ meat, warm pie—nice.
How can I account for it: he declares
he loves me. Why couldn't I have had *him*
in the beginning? Wind rageful. Sunday:
Good sermon. Olive in her new pink
checked shallie, me in black silk.
Washed my handkerchief
and neck ribbon. Monday: Must get work.
Tried seven places. Mailed my underteeth
to Dr. Drury to mend.
Mrs. Corbin gave sour milk and hard bread—
so thankful. Up early, incessant rain,
wood wet. Where is Mr. Lawson?
Secured a kitchen job 40 miles from town,
a hotel hosting two trains a day.
Wrote to John, heard not one word.
Does another woman lay claim to him?
$35 per month if I can stick to it.

Could not do the labor of three and please
so many, went to Webster, next stop up rail,
got work as laundress for Mrs. N
who read my fortune. *Sent 5 dollars
toward the house lien.* Wrote to John.
Will he come? Darned all evening, feel
the labor of yesterday's heavy wash *45 pieces*
for men from the charcoal kilns. Finally
a note from John, signed "very truly"
—not one word of love. Can Mrs. N read
his meaning? Ollie writes that she is ill, but Danny
able to put up lathing, though his eyes weak
from measles. God grant he finish
by winter. He's turned twelve, Ollie fifteen.
When will they have walls between rooms,
a heated home, the smell of coconut cake?
Sunday's sermon: The love of a pure woman is priceless.

Cut and worked buttonholes all day: 50 cents.
Mrs. N read my fortune.
I'm earning nothing but board,

how to cover my debts, buy lumber, pay
the plasterers? Fixed Mrs. N breakfast, carried slops.
Tired of doing without thanks.
Where is John Lawson? Why
do I love him so? Pure truths
the only words of value.

In my prayers this night: on my gravestone,
let *She Hath Done What She Could*
be my final accounting.

A Bridesmaid's Tale
Minnie Griffith Gupton, 1893

Remember the snowy day Miss Hammer
let us out of school early?
Older than our mothers, pretty strict, and not
at all pretty, for days she wore
the same dark dress covered
by voluminous faded aprons.
Two gunny bags hung
across her black saddle horse,
she left with our older classmates
walking in the railroad right-of-way direction.
You and I and the Gupton boys

headed for our playhouses.
Mine, a ring of shiny stones;
Yours, a few boxes, bits of china.
Skillfully I frosted mud pies
with milkweed. Your rag doll's children:
six borrowed clothespins with
dried hollyhock flower skirts.
We exchanged neighborly visits
while the Gupton brothers
stuck their hair full of feathers,
daubed colored chalk on each other's cheeks.
Nervous, we mimicked our mothers' chatter:
No nice woman allows a man,
not in the family,
to see baby before ten days of age.
No nice woman walks
in public places when
the coming event
casts its shadow before.

Mounted on broomstick horses
with embroidered cotton-stuffed sock heads,
the Gupton boys circled—
though we did not completely comprehend,
we continued: *No nice woman feeds baby*

from a bottle, a mark of vanity,
a mark of lack of love for her offspring.
No nice woman tells the secret
of her condition before the truth
becomes impossible to conceal.

With animal yells the Guptons charged
our playhouses.
We fled for our lives, woe
to the luckless doll
who fell into their hands: scalped,
torn limb from limb, then
stomped upon.

We buried our dead
in the snow where next we played
Valley Forge.
Beetpickle vinegar made
bloodstained tracks crossing
the Delaware. At Rock Creek
we captured Ticonderoga.
Digging up our dead dolls,
the Gupton boys played surgeon.
Attending the troops, they intoned:
fatty heart, hobnailed liver, death
from delirium tremens—not uncommon.

With the now unrecognizable dolls,
we watched from the benchland:
below us Miss Hammer rode the rail line
accompanied by our classmates,
a fresh tablecloth of snow pocked
by black holes. Scholars scrambled
from blemish to blemish, picking up
coal fallen from flatcars, helping teacher
fill her gunny bags with fuel to boil her dinner—
a crisp cabbage (the outer leaves
like starched petticoats) and four
fingerling potatoes. As part
of her pay, our fathers supplied hay
for Miss Hammer's well-muscled horse.

Turning their hands into firearms, the Gupton boys
shot their broomstick ponies
out from under one another. Remember?
How you and I shivered, cleaved
to each other, pondering the possibilities:
our lives as teachers—Miss Hammer—
or wives—the two Mrs. Guptons.

If No Impediment Shall Be Alleged
The Gift of Aunt Rebecca Miller, 1893

Hands joined, hands loosened—
the groom leaving a gold ring
on the fourth finger, left hand;
minister addressing those assembled...

An extravagance, everyone says,
given to me for my own betrothal:
dull black walnut sheen
perfect for its massive design,
headboard reaching to heaven
looming for years
in my parents' bed chamber,
dresser to match, like a portly wife
beside her ogre husband
snoring in the corner.
The dresser's top two
built-in chests fully equipped
with a false hair switch coiled
snakelike next to a lace-
trimmed chemise, handkerchiefs,
sachet, packet of pink
rice face powder.
An extravagance,
the headboard carved in one
circular design haloed by leaves—
in lamplight a leering Cyclops.
The wedding guests run
fingers over the sleigh-shaped footboard,
this cabinetmaker's art innocent
of metal attachments, a perfect marriage
of tongue and groove where every piece
holds another in place.
How it held when I wanted
to take it apart for spring cleaning,
six slats supporting springs notched
into side stays.
Tugging and sweating and calling it pet

names that would have blistered
its varnish if it had any.
As a child I recall
mother bossing father from the sidelines
until at last it fell like a house around us.
Steadfast as Gibraltar until it flew
into pieces for no reason
—maybe plummeting temperatures—
blasting its inhabitants from sleep.
The ponderous headboard threatening
to fall crushing Mr. Miller and myself—
a *damnfinemess*, extricating ourselves
from the shipwreck, husband swearing
to make kindling of it, in white night dresses
we looked like owls awakened from sleep.
Where had my parents gotten it—
along the trail west, left behind by travelers
to lighten their load? Extravagant,

the groom leaving a gold ring
on the fourth finger, minister addressing
family and neighbors.
Hands joined, hands loosened, joined again;
reverently discreetly advisedly soberly.
No impediment alleged
not even this gift of a bed. Amen
to that, author of life everlasting—

I'm rid of it.

Oh Promise Me

Hearing God's message while the organ rolls
Its mighty music to our very souls,
No love less perfect than a life with thee;
Oh, promise me! Oh, promise me!

Afterword

Unlike their mothers, many of the brides represented here worked outside of the home before they married, filling in as schoolteachers, laundresses, cooks, or clerks for men who had answered the call of mining, exploring, or soldiering. This was a group of women who for a few years made their own way and earned their own money (albeit about half of what men were paid for the same tasks), women who did not have to depend on a male relative for support. Further, beginning in 1850, for the first time in the history of the United States, a married woman could own property in her own name. These circumstances must have instilled in these young women, if not a new confidence, then a new worldview. It was a heady time in the history of North America, the smell of destiny was in the air and, because of this and the above mentioned, these new wives had wider horizons than their foremothers. Collectively, my frontier brides, including the nuns, seem to have been filled with even more expectations for the future than their female forebears but due to their isolation, displacement, and the lawlessness of the time, they also faced more peril.

In 1839, twenty-eight-year-old Lucy Thompson ("Typus Orbis Terrarum") had been acquainted with her new husband, the Reverend Jason Lee, only a few months when she left Newberry Seminary in Vermont and joined him, sailing around Cape Horn to his church's mission near the settlement of Salem in Oregon Country. The previous year, Reverend Lee's first wife had perished from complications of childbirth and was laid to rest in the same Willamette Valley grove where she had been married. In addition to meditations on the Bible, Lucy's main occupation during her ocean voyage was the study of Chinook jargon. Her mission in the West was to help her husband in shepherding sick Native American children to a "happy" Christian death.

Eleven years later, in 1850, Elizabeth Millar ("Cloth") graduated from Troy Seminary in New York and sailed west alone via the Isthmus of Panama. On her journey, she read *Women's Indispensable Assistant* and, though she had no groom in mind, shopped in Panama City for cloth and a pattern for her wedding gown. In Portland she wasn't surprised to discover a dreary village devoid of women except for a few schoolteachers like herself but was flabbergasted to be distained as an old maid at twenty-one.

On the trail west to Oregon in 1851, Martha Gay ("The Stove") and her older sister, Mamie, stopped to fish at a creek just off the Barlow Road. When they grew bored, the girls decided to inspect a nearby landmark, an iron stove discarded by an emigrant. Two drovers from another company of overlanders rode up with the same intent. One drover struck up a conversation with Mamie and professed that he would marry her. Though he rode away forgetting to ask Mamie her name, a year later he showed up at the Gay family's Eugene homestead and proposed to her.

In the spring of 1855, Elizabeth Shepard ("About These Trumpeters That Line My Walls") was only fourteen and motherless (and perhaps, in her father's estimation, taking up too much of her new stepmother's time) when her father informed her that the following week she would marry a man named Holtgrieve whom Elizabeth had met but once.

Sarah Givens ("On the Second Through Train") had a lengthy engagement; she hardly knew her father. He had married her mother after a brief courtship, then left New Harmony, Kansas, for the California gold fields a few months after Sarah was born in 1852, never to return. Seventeen years later, for Sarah's honeymoon trip just after the golden spike was driven on the transatlantic rail line, Sarah's new husband, a Civil War veteran named R. D. Jones, bought tickets to Sacramento on the second through train. He had a surprise for Sarah, a reunion with her father, whom Jones had located. The newlyweds found Mr. Givens, dissipated and living in squalor with a prostitute. Interviewed when she was a widow in her eighties, Sarah still keenly remembered her feelings of pity, shame, and disappointment.

And what of the indigenous women of the American West who were taken as brides by white men? Soldiers stationed on the frontier sometimes formed liaisons with tribal women, but if anything has been written by the Native Americans with whom Sherman, Grant, and possibly even Custer shared brief domestic arrangements, I have not been able to unearth them.

Most military men moved on without their Native female companions and with no further thought of them or their offspring. Others, such as a Portuguese sailor who had somehow attached himself to the British navy and was shipwrecked off the Oregon coast in the late 1860s, took Native wives they prized highly. In this particular case, the Portuguese, as he was known, founded a trading post with goods salvaged from the sea. When his Native wife died ("Kloh-Kloh"), he demanded a Catholic funeral. He buried her near his mercantile and, much to the consternation of the local white inhabitants, followed the custom of her people: He laid his wife to rest with her belongings, purportedly throwing into her grave every article from his store that she had coveted or admired—including a barrel of pastry flour and bolts of calico.

Because I've lived in the Northwest for much of my life, I chose subjects who emigrated there, then began to wonder if any of them ever met. As this manuscript began to take shape, I noticed connections between several of my new brides. Remarkably, I also noticed that fate had led a handful of these young women down paths that crossed mine. In 1849 both Marianne Hunsaker's ("The Doll") and Lucy Ann Henderson's ("Lucy Ann Shows Off her Scrapbook and Talks about the Art of Regulating Temperatures") fathers had been swept up by the gold rush. Six-year-old Marianne was placed in a boarding school run by the Quebecois Sisters of Notre Dame in Oregon City, while a few blocks away fourteen-year-old Lucy Ann enrolled as a new student at Mrs. Thornton's boarding school. It was here that Lucy met her future husband, Judge Matthew P. Deady, when he acted as a messenger bearing Lucy notes from an admirer. Many years later, my family moved near Oregon City. Attending the University of Oregon, I studied mathematics in the institution's oldest building, named for Lucy's husband. It was while reading an interview of Lucy that I first came across the quote used as the title of this book—you haven't asked me about my wedding or what I wore—and have I come across many variations of this quote since.

In 1849, Marianne Hunsaker's father and mother went in search of fortune, milling lumber to be shipped to San Francisco, the proceeds of which funded a homestead on the Clackamas River near Oregon City. In an interview of Marianne conducted by Fred Lockley and published in the *Oregon Journal* in 1922, I came across another quote that echoed throughout my reading: "My mother bore twelve children, worked hard all her life, and died a comparatively young woman. It usually was the second or third wife

Sarah Jane Sturgess Anderson's wedding dress, 1851.

that enjoyed the improved farm and the comforts that the first and second wives had worked so hard to help earn." Marianne Hunsaker Edwards D'Arcy became the first secretary of the Women's Suffrage Party in Oregon; Abigail Scott Duniway was president. I did not write about Abigail, a novelist and journalist who wrote poignantly about her own experiences, but I never forgot something that I read about her youth: She saved for a year from her meager wages at her first job as a schoolteacher to buy her wedding dress.

When I was well into the writing of this collection, I discovered that one of my brides did indeed cross paths with another. On June 17, 1866, Elizabeth Paschal Dillon ("The Widow, Her Song without Words, sans Piano") married Martin Gay, brother of Martha and Maime Gay ("The Stove"). In Martha Gay Masterson's recollections of her life, settling what was then called the Northwest Country, she mentioned that her brother married Elizabeth Dillon (born 1838), "a sweet-voiced widow" with a little girl. I had written about Elizabeth and knew that she was not a widow but a woman who had divorced her hopelessly alcoholic husband, a surgeon, Dr. A.R. Dillon. I don't know who authored this piece of misinformation—Martin Gay certainly knew Elizabeth's circumstances; he had met her husband in the gold fields. Given the stigma of divorce and the difficulty of acquiring a dissolution of marriage at the time, I have come to suspect that more than one nineteenth-century "widow" in the American West was really a divorcée who took on widowhood as a polite façade.

Elizabeth Paschal had married her first husband on December 4, 1859, in Virginia. When Elizabeth, Dr. Dillon, and their baby daughter crossed the plains in 1862, they headed for Auburn, a mining boomtown on Elkhorn Ridge in the Blue Mountains of eastern Oregon. During the winter of 1862–1863, as Auburn's population grew from nothing to more than five thousand inhabitants, Elizabeth Dillon's husband plied his surgical skills on injured miners and sawyers and, according to his wife, began to drink heavily. Elizabeth, whose father had also been a doctor, sometimes assisted as his nurse.

Cynthia Abrams Stafford ("Cynthia, Cyrus Stafford's First Wife") was born near Potsdam, New York, in 1835 (the same year as Lucy Henderson and Catherine Sager). When she and her husband crossed the plains as newlyweds, they departed from Iowa in the same year as Elizabeth Dillon and her first husband and also trekked to Auburn to seek their fortune. The Staffords' plan was to strike it rich, then to return to Potsdam with enough money to buy a farm. Cyrus mined; Cynthia, who had attended Mt. Holyoke, taught school. In fact, both Cynthia and Elizabeth had taught school in Iowa before they went west.

In March of 1863 when Cynthia fell seriously ill from exposure and overwork, was she treated by the dipsomaniacal Dr. Dillon? Or had he already fled—possibly in the same party of miners as Cynthia's husband—to the more promising gold fields in Boise Basin? Did Elizabeth and Cynthia ever meet? According to Elizabeth, her husband spent all of his earnings at the saloon and in order to support herself and her baby, she took in laundry. In mining camps where the male population was occupied with the possibility of acquiring overnight fortune, the job of mortician often fell to the laundress. Was it Elizabeth who laid Cynthia out after she died alone in her pine hut on March 24, 1863? I stumbled over this possible connection after I had written about Elizabeth and while I was writing about Cynthia. I had become interested in Cynthia because she was the first wife of Cyrus Stafford, who became a prominent judge in Northern California. According to an article written by Cynthia's great-great-grandniece, the historian Virginia Duffy McLoughlin, and published in the *Oregon Historical Quarterly*, when Judge Stafford's biography was written, any mention of a marriage to Cynthia Abrams was completely omitted.

So many of my subjects had Iowa and New York in their background that I began to think of these states as a common thread between the brides and grooms whose lives I recorded here. Elizabeth Millar Wilson ("Cloth") came west from New York as did Ida Mae Hallock Dutton's family ("Ida Mae Recalls the Broken Plates of her China Anniversary"); Cynthia Stafford was a native of New York State. Sarah Jane Sturgess ("An Answer for Mr. Anderson") and her family were from New York as was Lucy Thompson's family. Though both Mother Joseph ("The Brides of Christ Consider the Hunger…") and Mother Veronica ("The Matter of the Raspberries") grew up in rural Quebec, they each came west by ship after lengthy stays in convents in New York City. Before she took her final vows, Mother Veronica spent a year in New York State in the home of an older brother who had fled British sanctions after participating in a French Canadian uprising.

My Quebecois nuns had been missioned to the Northwest by their bishop in order to minister to the families of French Canadian trappers. These two nuns seem to have had an amicable working relationship with each other; one the head of a teaching order in Oregon, the other the head of a healing order across the Columbia River in Washington Territory.

Neither of these religious women volunteered to leave her country or the mother house of her newly organized religious order, and I doubt that either of them was anything but thunderstruck to be sent so far from home. It should be noted that some of the other women and children mentioned in these dramatic monologues also might have been somewhat less than thrilled about being resettled in the West.

But come they did. And if my brides or their families did not come west by ship, departing from New York harbor, then Iowa as a jumping-off place seems to have been a common denominator among them. Elizabeth Shepard Holtgrieve came across the plains from Rome, Iowa, in 1852, the year after her German mother died. Her father had emigrated to the Midwest from New York. As mentioned, Cynthia Stafford and Elizabeth Dillon both taught school in Iowa. Before she moved to Denver, Emily French ("Brown Cloth-Covered Diary of Memoranda & Cash Accounts") was a longtime resident of Iowa.

Finally, there was a contingent of brides with origins in the slave-owning South. In 1844, the Sager sisters ("Considering Her Answer to a Letter Sent by Emigrant" and "Brother Churchianity's Garden") came west across Iowa with their parents from the neighboring state of Missouri as did Lucy Ann Henderson's family in 1846 and Kate Thomas Morris's ("Lament of the Slatted Sunbonnets") family in 1851. Amanda Gardener Johnson ("Gifted to Miss Lydia Corum upon her Marriage to Anderson Deckard"), a slave, was brought west in 1853 from Missouri by her owners, who originated in Kentucky. In 1846 Marianne Hunsaker's family emigrated from just to the east of Iowa, in Illinois; her parents had both grown up on plantations in Kentucky. Reverend Jones ("How We Got On") came west from Illinois in 1853 with his parents, both of whom were born on Southern plantations.

There is a woman, Marilla Anderson Gardner, born in Washington Territory into a family who emigrated from New York, whom I did not write about, though her story continues to haunt me. I have a photograph of Marilla at her fiftieth wedding anniversary celebrated in 1928 in Hazel Dell, Washington. She is handsome, taller than her husband, who is twelve years her senior; she still has a head of thick, dark hair, which is fashionably bobbed. Her neck juts like a long-stemmed lily from her strong, square shoulders. Marilla's hands appear manlike; in them she clutches a bouquet of dark roses. In this photo she wears her mother's silk wedding dress, which Marilla wore as a bride of eighteen in 1878. Marilla's mother, Sarah Jane Sturgess Anderson, also wore this dress to her fiftieth wedding celebration in 1901. It is Sarah Jane ("An Answer for Mr. Anderson") about whom I wrote, largely because, in a reminiscence authored by Marilla Gardner, Marilla speaks volumes about her mother's life and very little about her own.

In 1847 at the age of nine, Sarah Jane came across the plains from New York with her parents and two younger siblings, arriving in Portland just after what came to be called the Whitman Massacre. After crossing the Snake River in what is now Idaho, their overland party had separated, some having gone to winter at the Whitman Mission near Walla Walla. There, on November 29, 1847, all but one of the men at the settlement were killed, most of the women and children taken hostage. Sarah Jane was a contemporary of the Sager sisters, who lived at the mission at the time of the murders and about whom I have written. Catherine Sager, the eldest sister, was especially well known throughout the territory, because, despite her tender age, she was called as a witness at the trial of the five Cayuse Indians accused of the crime. I have often wondered if Sarah Jane's path and the Sager girls' (Catherine, Elizabeth, Matilda, and Henrietta Naomi) ever crossed.

News of the Whitman Massacre galvanized the nation. In 1836 Narcissa and Marcus Whitman had been sent west by the American Board of Commissioners of Foreign Missions to convert the Cayuse and Umatilla Indians. Their mission, Waiilatpu, was located near Fort Walla Walla on the Walla Walla River, a tributary of the Columbia. After about eight years, the Cayuse and Umatilla became angered by the growing number of white emigrants pouring into their country, many of whom stopped at the Waiilatpu settlement, either for supplies or for the winter. The emigrants brought measles and other diseases to which the Native Americans had no immunity. Though the indigenous population was nursed by Dr. Whitman (a minister who had taken a "medical course"), they perished by the hundreds. Children were especially vulnerable. These particular tribes held that a shaman who attended to a sick person but did not cure him could be killed.

According to Catherine Sager, when Catholic priests arrived in this part of Oregon Country and tried to convert the Native Americans to Catholicism, the Natives became confused and angered by the conflicting Christian doctrines. On the morning of November 29, 1847, tensions came to a head. A half-Indian from Canada named Joe Lewis, who was wintering at Waiilatpu, began inciting a group of young local tribesman to violence. Before the day was over thirteen were dead. Marcus Whitman, age forty-three, was tomahawked in the head; Narcissa, age thirty-nine, was shot, allegedly by Joe Lewis. Eleven others, including Catherine's two older teenage brothers, were murdered. Fifty-four women and children, including Catherine and her sisters, were taken hostage and held for a month until they were ransomed by the Hudson Bay Company at Fort Vancouver. Several of the children, including Catherine's younger sister Hannah, died of measles during captivity. The nation was outraged. The massacre brought about the Cayuse War and prompted Congress in 1848 to create the Oregon Territory. In 1850 five men, all Cayuse Indians, were tried in Oregon City, found guilty of the murders, and, despite the fact that it was suspected that many of the witnesses were not at the scene of the crime, publicly hanged. Joe Lewis was not one of them.

In the early autumn of 1847, a few days before he and his family would have arrived at the Whitman Mission where they planned to refresh their supplies, Sarah Jane Sturgess's father, Moses Sturgess, drowned trying to ford his cattle across the Snake River. I read about this tragedy in the reminiscence written by Marilla Gardner and again came across a mention of it in Elizabeth Dixon Smith's overland diary collected, ed-ited, and annotated by Kenneth Holmes in the first volume of *Covered Wagon Women* (Bison Books, 1995). In Oregon City in 1848, Sarah Jane's widowed mother, Elizabeth Weldon Jennings Sturgess, married Moses Kellogg, who had come overland on the same wagon train as the Stur-gesses. It wasn't a happy union, however; the pair fought and eventually Kellogg died or deserted Elizabeth and their infant. Shortly thereafter, at the age of thirteen and a half, Sarah Jane married William Reese Anderson and the newlyweds claimed a plot of land near a tributary of the Cowlitz River near Fort Vancouver in what is now Washington State. Both mother and daughter appear to have been land brides, their mar-riages facilitating their husbands' ability to claim up to 640 acres (twice the amount of land the provisional government accorded to a single man) through, in Elizabeth's case, the Organic Act and, in Sarah's case, the Donation Land Claim Act of 1850. While thirteen seems too tender an age for marriage, it wasn't unusual, and in my research I came across mention of land brides as shockingly young as eleven. This latter law, the Donation Land Claim Act, was one of the first that allowed married women in the United States to own property under their own name. (Interestingly, the Donation Land Act did not apply to Native American women, unless they were half white.) Sarah Jane and William Anderson lived on 320 acres where William, a government scout, mountain man, and fur trapper, eventually worked as a bucket maker probably for the sugar beet trade, constructing hoops from native hazelnut. Part of their homestead became the community of Hazel Dell.

I tried to imagine Sarah Jane and her mother in 1851, shopping for cloth for Sarah's wedding dress at the Hudson Bay Company store at Fort Vancouver, located on the north shore of the Columbia River across from the tiny village of Portland—still known by most locals as Middletown (or Mudtown), because it lay on the Willamette River between Oregon City and the Fort. Though the Hudson Bay Company no longer operated under the auspices of the British government, English influences prevailed. Listening to the shopkeeper expound upon Queen Victoria's white wedding as he pointed to illustrations of the young queen in women's magazines, mother and daughter choose a pale Chinese silk in windowpane plaid and a modest but imperial-looking pattern. That very night the women began cutting and hand stitching Sarah Jane's gown: a high V-neck, above-the-elbow cuffed bell sleeves, the long skirt gathered just above the natural waist. As she stitched, did Sarah Jane dream that she would one day have a daughter who would wear that same dress, that this gown would be serviceable well into the twentieth century, that her daughter would brag at her golden wedding anniversary celebration that it hadn't a hole? Indeed, could Sarah Jane—who was known as Janey to relatives—have fathomed that her great-great-granddaughter would one day wear this dress before it was donated to a museum?

In the mid-1860s, when the older part of Fort Vancouver was torn down and some of the lumber scavenged by Mother Joseph to build the territory's first and, for a long time, only hospital, did Sarah Jane's husband, whose livelihood depended on his talent with wood, marvel at Mother Joseph's knowledge of lumber learned at the knee of her carriage-maker father? Did Sarah Jane's husband ever watch this nun, a hammer secured around her waist by means of a rope, inspect the workers' progress, redoing the handiwork that didn't meet with her approval? Was anyone from Sarah Jane's family ever treated at the Sisters of Providence hospital headed by Mother Joseph, a woman who was not an American citizen and who spoke only a few words of English?

When Sarah Jane came to Hazel Dell as a child bride, her only near neighbors were Native Americans. Like Lucy Thompson Lee before her, Sarah Jane was well versed in the trade jargon of Chinook, a pidgin of mostly English, French, and several Indian dialects. Her new home was so isolated that, according to her daughter, she claimed to have for a time forgotten how to speak English. Sarah Jane bore fourteen children, thirteen of whom survived to adulthood. According to Marilla, she named several of her sons for important American military figures: William Franklin, George Washington, Edward Doncarlos Buell, and Robert E. Lee. Marilla, Sarah Jane's oldest daughter, was born in 1860 and never lived more than twenty miles from her birthplace. (I have often wondered about the origins of this child's name; was she named for a hamlet in New York State near Sarah Jane Sturgess' birthplace?) Marilla's husband, whose profession I never learned, died in 1936. In her later years, when Marilla began hiring taxis to visit long-deceased friends, she was moved to a nursing home. Together with a younger retired male resident, Marilla escaped over a chain link fence and camped in the woods near where her mother had lived as a bride of thirteen and a half. The pair's whereabouts went undiscovered for two weeks. When they were found, it was reported that Marilla was anything but delighted to be rescued.

You Haven't Asked Me about My Wedding or What I Wore: Poems of Courtship on the North American Frontier follows in the tradition of three of my previous books of poetry. *Oh How Can I Keep on Singing? Voices of Pioneer Women* (Ontario Review Press, 1993) is a collection of linked poems that concern the women who lived in or emigrated to the Okanogan Valley in Washington Territory when it was opened up for white settlement in the late 1880s. *The Dust of Everyday Life: An Epic Poem of the Pacific Northwest* (Sasquatch Books, 1997) concerns the families of two immigrant children who met and married. *We Never Speak of It: Idaho-Wyoming Poems, 1889–90* (Ontario Review Press, 2003) is framed by one academic year in the life of a schoolteacher in a high-desert town near the Idaho-Wyoming border. All of these books represent a confluence of historical narrative and poetic imagery written out of what has come to be called the documentary imagination.

Like my other books of verse, the dramatic monologues in *You Haven't Asked Me About My Wedding or What I Wore* were informed by my travels, historical documents, and archival materials, including photographs, diaries, journals, household and personal artifacts, newspapers, letters, reminiscences, interviews, obituaries, cookbooks, maps, songs, scrapbooks, and whatever else might ink the pen. These dramatic monologues—part biography, part history, and part invented memoir—are my interpretations of how "average" nineteenth-century women and children felt about matters of courtship and marriage. I see this work of recovered history depicting the minutia of North American frontier life as a supplement to conventional history texts. My hope is that others will also.

≈⟁≈

Lucy Thompson, b. 1818, New York
Fidelia Munson, b. 1819
Granny Wintersteen, b. 1825
Mother Veronica of the Crucifix (Hedwidge Onesime Davignon),
    b. 1820, Québec
Mother Joseph of the Sacred Heart (Esther Pariseau),
    b.1823, Québec
Elizabeth Millar Wilson, b. 1830, New York
Mary Hallen, b. 1832
Amanda Gardener Johnson, b. 1833, Missouri
Catherine Sager, b. 1835, Missouri
Lucy Ann Henderson Deady, b. 1835, Missouri
Cynthia Abrams Stafford, b. 1835, New York
Elizabeth Paschal Dillon Gay, b. 1838, Virginia
Sarah Jane Sturgess Anderson, b. 1838, New York
Matilda Sager Delaney, b. 1839, Missouri
Elizabeth Shepard Holtgrieve, b. 1840, Iowa
Kate Thomas, b. 1841, Missouri
Marianne D'Arcy, b. 1841, Missouri
Reverend T. L. Jones, b. 1841, Illinois
Emily French, b. 1843
Sarah Ann Givens Jones, b. 1852, Kansas
South Wind, b. ca. 1860, Oregon
Belle Bishop, b. ca. 1860
Ida Mae Dutton, b. 1860, Oregon
Marilla Anderson Gardner, b. 1860, Washington Territory
Minnie Griffith Gupton, b. 1873

≈⟁≈

Acknowledgments

It would be nearly impossible to thank the many, many people who helped me during the ten years it took to bring this book to light, but I'll try. First, thanks to my tribe: for her undying faith in my work, my agent, Robin Straus; for their expertise and help with research, my friends since high school Don Blanchard, MD, and Mary Brandon; to my college roommate Kathryn Ellingson, who has read and commented on every poem I have ever written; to my husband Mark Bothwell, for his patience and his technical advice; to my readers Karl Garson, Joan Maiers, Leigh Bienen, Henry Bienen, Raymond Smith, Joyce Carol Oates, and Maxine Kumin. Thanks also to Susan Hunter for her stories and expertise; to the Oregon Historical Society's Scott Root and Scott Daniels; and to Suze Hammond for her family history, historical photographs, and eye for detail. A thousand thanks to Jean M. Ward. Finally, to my truly inspired gem-of-an-editor, James Engelhardt, a really big "Thank You" for your incredible vision.

Thanks also the editors of the following journals where some of these poems previously appeared:

"The Gift of a Found Half Moon": *Court Green*
"Typus Orbis Terrarum": *Boulevard*
"Considering Her Answer to a Letter Sent By Emigrant": *Feminist Studies*
"Cloth": *Boulevard*
"The Doll": *Court Green*
"The Stove": *Mipoesias*

"Brother Churchianity's Garden": *TriQuarterly*

"That Long Looked For Day": *Michigan Quarterly Review*

"Cynthia, Cyrus Stafford's First Wife": *Mipoesias*

"About These Trumpeters That Line My Walls": *Long Journey: Contemporary Northwest Poets* (edited by David Biespiel. Corvallis: Oregon State University Press, 2006)

"The Brides of Christ Consider the Hunger...": *TriQuarterly*

"The Widow, Her Song without Words, sans Piano": *Michigan Quarterly Review*

"The Matter of the Raspberries": *TriQuarterly*

"The Grass Hunter": *Ontario Review*

"On the Second through Train": *Feminist Studies*

"The Gift of Granny Wintersteen": *Feminist Studies*

"Cutting Her Out from the Flock": *Long Journey: Contemporary Northwest Poets* (edited by David Biespiel Corvallis: Oregon State University Press, 2006)

"A Good Many Brides Today Are a Pampered Self-Indulgent Lot": *Kalliope*

"You Haven't Asked Me About My Wedding or What I Wore": first appeared as part of *The Dust of Everyday Life: An Epic Poem of the Northwest* (Seattle: Sasquatch Books, 1997)

"If No Impediment Shall Be Alleged": *Court Green*

Notes on Hymns, Music, and Lyrics

And though this world, with devils filled, should threaten to undo us;
We will not fear, for God hath willed His truth to triumph through us.

From the hymn "A Mighty Fortress is Our God" ("Ein feste Burg ist unser Gott"). Words and music by Martin Luther, 1529. First translated into English by Myles Coverdale in 1539.

~❦~

There is a place where Jesus sheds
The oil of gladness on our heads;
From every stormy wind that blows,
From every swelling tide of woes,
There is a calm, a sure retreat;
'Tis found beneath the mercy seat.

From the hymn "From Every Stormy Wind That Blows". Words by Hugh Stowell, 1831.

~❦~

"Jésus et Marie, Ma Force et Ma Gloire"
(Jesus and Mary, my strength and my glory)

Motto of the Sisters of the Holy Names of Jesus and Mary, (Soeurs des Saints Noms de Jésus et de Marie), founded 1843, Longueuil, Quebec, Canada.

~❦~

Je Mets Ma Confiance
Ja mets ma confiance,
Vierge, en votre secours.
Servez-moi de défense,
Prenez soin de mes jours.

My Trust Lies in You
I place my trust in your help,
O Virgin.
Be my defense,
Watch over all of my days

Words attributed to founder of the Daughters of Wisdom, St. Louis-Marie Grignion de Montfort of Brittany, circa 1800. Translation: anonymous.

~❦~

At First, Judge Bacon was Reluctant to allow his Daughter Libbie to be Courted by the Son of the Blacksmith, (*The Custer Story: The Life and Intimate Letters of George A. Custer and His Wife Elizabeth*. Ed. Marguerite Merington. New York: Devin-Adair Company, 1950): Letters, page 76, 82–83.

❦

When through the deep waters I call thee to go,
The rivers of woe shall not thee overflow;

That soul, though all hell should endeavor to shake,
I'll never, no never no never forsake.

From the hymn "How Firm A Foundation." Words attributed to various authors, 1787.

❦

I fear no foe, with Thee at hand to bless:
Ills have no weight, and tears no bitterness:
Where is death's sting? Where, grave, they victory?
I triumph still, if Thou abide with me.

From the hymn "Abide with Me." Words by Henry F. Lyte, 1847, music "Eventide" by William H. Monk, 1861.

❦

Hearing God's message while the organ rolls
Its mighty music to our very souls,
No love less perfect than a life with thee;
Oh, promise me! Oh, promise me!

From "Oh Promise Me." Lyrics by Clement Scott. Published 1889, Schirmer, Inc.

❦